Ilene Bartos

Spectacular
RECTANGLES

12 Quilts from a Simple Shape

Martingale®
& COMPANY

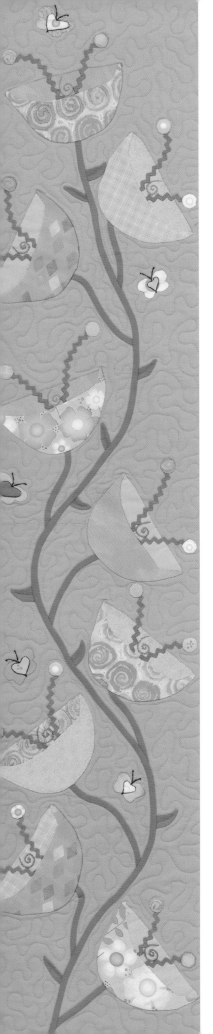

Spectacular Rectangles: 12 Quilts from a Simple Shape
©2010 by Ilene Bartos

That Patchwork Place® is an imprint
of Martingale & Company®.

Martingale & Company
20205 144th Ave. NE
Woodinville, WA 98072-8478 USA
www.martingale-pub.com

Printed in China
15 14 13 12 11 10   8 7 6 5 4 3 2 1

Library of Congress Cataloging-in-Publication Data
Library of Congress Control Number: 2009038355

ISBN: 978-1-56477-935-9

MISSION STATEMENT
Dedicated to providing quality products and service to inspire creativity.

CREDITS
President & CEO ▪ Tom Wierzbicki
Editor in Chief ▪ Mary V. Green
Managing Editor ▪ Tina Cook
Developmental Editor ▪ Karen Costello Soltys
Technical Editor ▪ Ellen Pahl
Copy Editor ▪ Melissa Bryan
Design Director ▪ Stan Green
Production Manager ▪ Regina Girard
Illustrator ▪ Adrienne Smitke
Cover & Text Designer ▪ Regina Girard
Photographer ▪ Brent Kane

CONTENTS

INTRODUCTION

A myriad of shapes are used in quiltmaking, but squares and rectangles are the most common ones in pieced quilts. Quilt blocks are usually finished to be squares so they will fit together nicely, often with sashing or setting blocks. Most finished quilts end up being either square or rectangular, with a few circular ones thrown into the mix.

I wanted to see if I could design a group of quilts using only rectangular blocks and challenged myself to explore various ways of setting them together. At first, my designs begin simply as a drawing, a glimmer of an idea or a figment of my imagination. Until I've found the colors and fabrics to make my quilts complete, my designs aren't real to me. Once it has been pieced together and quilted, a quilt becomes real—a true and faithful friend. I'm not sure how this happens, but I believe it's why quilts offer such great comfort and love to the people who use them. They become our friends, sharing in our joys and sadness, and they somehow miraculously manage to do this while remaining inanimate objects.

Working with rectangles was a fun experiment for me, and I believe I came up with some unexpected and unusual designs that I hope you will enjoy. Some of the quilts are set together in rows using traditional construction, while others are easily assembled using partial seams. These "friends" I'm sharing with you turned out to be much more powerful than the original drawings, and they are a special delight to me. I hope you enjoy working with rectangles as much as I do—and may the quilts you make with these patterns become real to you, providing joy, love, and comfort for you, your family, and your friends for years to come.

SAFARI

Designed and quilted by Ilene Bartos. Pieced by Jan Hall, Des Moines, Iowa.
Finished Quilt: 69½" x 75½" ▪ Finished Block: 3" x 6"

This is a dramatic quilt done with a variety of prints that bring to mind the animals you might see on an African safari. When looking at this design you won't immediately see the rectangles; once pieced into the vertical rows, the rectangular blocks are camouflaged within the overall pattern.

MATERIALS

All yardages are based on 42"-wide fabric.

½ yard *each* of 8 medium to dark background fabrics for quilt center and middle border

⅜ yard *each* of 8 light safari prints for quilt center and middle border

2 yards of solid black fabric for inner border, outer border, and binding

4¾ yards of fabric for backing

76" x 82" piece of batting

CUTTING

From each safari print, cut:
- 3 strips, 3½" x 42"; crosscut into 18 rectangles, 3½" x 6½"

From each dark background fabric, cut:
- 4 strips, 3½" x 42"; crosscut into 36 squares, 3½" x 3½"

From the solid black fabric, cut:
- 13 strips, 3½" x 42"
- 8 binding strips, 2½" x 42"

MAKING THE BLOCKS

The center of the quilt consists of eight vertical rows. To make construction easier, first decide which safari print will be used for each row, beginning on the left. Label the prints with row numbers 1 through 8. There are two different background fabrics used with each safari print, one on each side of the print. Decide where the background fabrics will go, placing them between your safari prints and numbering them 1 through 8. I suggest using the darkest fabric on the outer edges of rows 1 and 8. Each of the other fabrics will be used in two adjacent rows. I used progressively lighter fabrics toward the center of the quilt. Refer to the quilt diagram on page 11 as needed.

1. Begin with the row 1 safari print and the background that will be on the left. Draw a diagonal line on the wrong side of nine 3½" background squares. Draw a second line ½" from the first line and closer to the corner as shown.

2. Place one square on the left end of a row 1 safari print 3½" x 6½" rectangle right sides together, orienting it as shown. Sew on both drawn lines. Cut between the two sewing lines to form a 2¾" triangle square and a rectangle unit. Press the seam allowances on both units toward the dark fabric. Trim points on the triangle square and set it aside for later. Repeat to make nine.

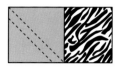 

Make 9 of each.

3. Using nine of the 3½" background squares that will be on the right side of row 1, repeat steps 1 and 2 to complete the unit and make additional 2¾" triangle squares. You will make nine rectangle units and a total of 18 triangle squares.

Make 18.   Make 9.

4. Using the same dark backgrounds on the left and the right, and the same safari print, repeat steps 1 through 3, rotating the diagonal seams in the opposite direction as shown. Press the seam allowances toward the safari print. Make nine rectangle units and 18 triangle squares.

Make 18.   Make 9.

5. Repeat the steps for each of the eight vertical rows, making nine units of each angle (18 total) and a total of 36 triangle squares for each row.

ASSEMBLING THE VERTICAL ROWS

1. Sew the row 1 safari print units together in pairs as shown to make a 6½" square. Make nine pieced squares. Press the seam allowances downward.

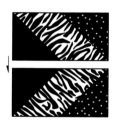 

Make 9.

2. Sew the nine pairs together to complete row 1; press the seam allowances downward.

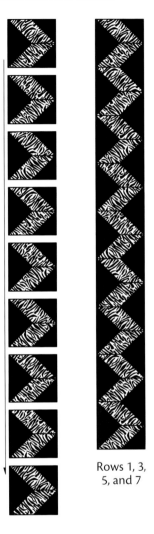

Rows 1, 3, 5, and 7

3. Repeat steps 1 and 2 for rows 3, 5, and 7.

4. For row 2, sew the safari print units in pairs going the opposite direction as shown, and press the seam allowances upward. Make nine pieced squares.

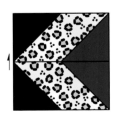

Make 9.

5. Sew the nine pairs together to complete row 2; press the seam allowances upward.

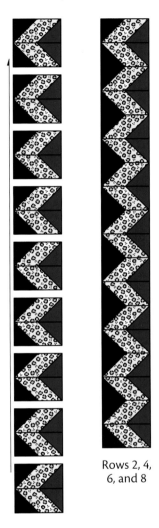

Rows 2, 4, 6, and 8

6. Repeat steps 4 and 5 for rows 4, 6, and 8.

7. Sew the eight vertical rows together to complete the quilt top. The top should measure 48½" x 54½".

ADDING THE INNER BORDERS

1. Refer to "Measuring Borders" on page 75. Measure, piece, and cut two 3½"-wide inner-border strips and sew them to the side edges of the quilt top. Press the seam allowances toward the border.

2. Measure, piece, and cut two 3½"-wide inner-border strips. Sew these to the top and bottom edges of the quilt top. Press the seam allowances toward the border.

MAKING THE PIECED BORDERS

1. Arrange four matching triangle squares so that the dark background is in the center as shown. Sew the squares together to make a 5" x 5" border block. Repeat to make 52 using a variety of the previously made triangle squares. You will have more triangle squares than needed.

Make 52.

BE CHOOSY

If you use two triangle squares from the safari units that are sewn in one direction and two from safari units sewn in the opposite direction, the seam allowances will snuggle together. You can also simply re-press the seam allowances as needed.

2. For the side borders, arrange 12 border blocks in a row, placing the lightest colors in the center and the darkest colors on the ends. Sew together, pressing the seam allowances in one direction. Make two.

Make 2.

3. From the leftover inner-border strips, cut four rectangles, 3½" x 5". Sew one on each end of the side border strips. Press the seam allowances toward the black.

Make 2.

4. Sew the side border strips to the side edges of the quilt top. Press the seam allowances toward the inner border.

5. For the top and bottom borders, arrange and sew 14 border blocks together, placing the lightest colors in the center and the darkest on the ends. Make two.

Make 2.

6. Sew the pieced border strips to the top and bottom edges of the quilt top. Press the seam allowances toward the inner border.

ADDING THE OUTER BORDER

1. Measure, piece, and cut two black 3½"-wide outer-border strips and sew them to the side edges of the quilt top. Press the seam allowances toward the outer border.

2. Measure, piece, and cut two black 3½"-wide outer-border strips for the top and bottom edges. Sew them to the quilt top and press the seam allowances toward the outer border.

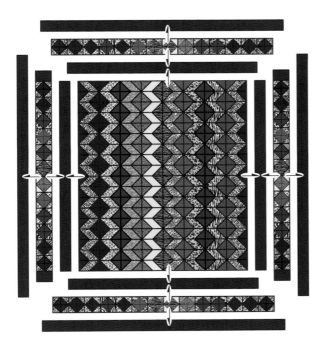

FINISHING THE QUILT

Refer to "Quiltmaking Basics" on page 76 as needed to complete the following steps.

1. Make a backing 3" to 5" larger on all sides than your quilt top.

2. Layer the quilt top with the batting and backing. Baste the layers together.

3. Quilt by hand or machine using the design of your choice.

4. Square up the quilt.

5. Prepare the binding and sew it to the quilt.

6. Add a label and a hanging sleeve, if desired, to complete your quilt.

QUILTING SUGGESTION

This design is a curl with spikes added to the outside curve. It is stitched in a row on the borders and more free-form throughout the center of the quilt.

ZIGGY ZAGGY

Designed and made by Ilene Bartos.

Finished Quilt: 76½" x 84" ▪ Finished Block: 8½" x 12"

This quilt is concocted of yummy browns with a touch of blue thrown in for fun. The design combines neutral colors with a bold, graphic look to appeal to the man in your life, but made in a different color scheme with floral fabrics, juvenile prints, or polka dots, it can easily be tailored to suit anyone perfectly.

MATERIALS

All yardages are based on 42"-wide fabric. Each vertical row uses four color-coordinated fabrics plus a blue for the block centers. The same four fabrics are used in two vertical rows—one with A and B blocks with dark fabrics in the center and a second row with C and D blocks with lights in the center. One vertical row (the middle row of the quilt shown) is made only once of A and B blocks and requires less fabric. This is designated as the fifth fabric set for the fifth A-B row.

½ yard *each* of 5 different dark fabrics for blocks

⅝ yard *each* of 4 different medium dark fabrics for blocks

¼ yard of a 5th medium dark fabric for A-B blocks

⅝ yard *each* of 4 different medium light fabrics for blocks

⅜ yard of a 5th medium light fabric for A-B blocks

½ yard *each* of 4 different light fabrics for blocks

⅛ yard of a 5th light fabric for A-B blocks

¼ yard *total* or scraps of assorted blue fabrics for block centers

1 yard of blue fabric for binding*

7½ yards of fabric for backing

82" x 90" piece of batting

*I made an extra-wide binding because I wanted it to be approximately the same width as the blue block centers, about ½" wide. If you want a narrower binding, ¾ yard will be enough.

CUTTING

From the assorted blue fabrics, cut:
- 63 rectangles 1" x 2"

From each of the 4 light fabrics, cut:
- 4 strips, 3" x 42"; crosscut into 7 rectangles, 3" x 6½", and 7 rectangles, 3" x 12½"
- 2 strips, 1½" x 42"; crosscut into 14 rectangles, 1½" x 2", and 7 rectangles, 1½" x 3"

From the 5th light fabric, cut:
- 2 strips, 1½" x 42"; crosscut into 14 rectangles, 1½" x 2", and 7 rectangles, 1½" x 3"

From each of the 4 medium dark fabrics, cut:
- 4 strips, 2½" x 42"; crosscut into 14 rectangles, 2½" x 4½", and 7 rectangles, 2½" x 10"
- 3 strips, 2" x 42"; crosscut into 14 rectangles, 2" x 3", and 7 rectangles, 2" x 6"

From the 5th medium dark fabric, cut:
- 3 strips, 2" x 42"; crosscut into 14 rectangles, 2" x 3", and 7 rectangles, 2" x 6"

From each of the 4 medium light fabrics, cut:
- 4 strips, 2½" x 42"; crosscut into 14 rectangles, 2½" x 4½", and 7 rectangles, 2½" x 10"
- 3 strips, 2" x 42"; crosscut into 14 rectangles, 2" x 3", and 7 rectangles, 2" x 6"

From the 5th medium light fabric, cut:
- 4 strips, 2½" x 42"; crosscut into 14 rectangles, 2½" x 4½", and 7 rectangles, 2½" x 10"

From each of 4 dark fabrics, cut:
- 4 strips, 3" x 42"; crosscut into 7 rectangles, 3" x 6½", and 7 rectangles, 3" x 12½"
- 2 strips, 1½" x 42"; crosscut into 14 rectangles, 1½" x 2", and 7 rectangles, 1½" x 3"

From the 5th dark fabric, cut:
- 4 strips, 3" x 42"; crosscut into 7 rectangles, 3" x 6½", and 7 rectangles, 3" x 12½"

From the blue fabric for binding, cut:
- 9 strips, 3½" x 42"

MAKING THE A AND B BLOCK ROWS

1. Choose one set of four fabrics—a light, a medium dark, a medium light, and a dark—to make one vertical row at a time. Arrange a blue 1" x 2" rectangle between two light 1½" x 2" rectangles as shown. Sew together, pressing the seam allowances toward the center. Add a light 1½" x 3" rectangle to the left side of the unit, pressing the seam allowances toward the light rectangle. Make seven.

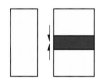

Make 7.

2. Sew medium dark 2" x 3" rectangles to both the top and bottom of the unit. Press the seam allowances toward the center. Sew a medium dark 2" x 6" rectangle to the left side of the unit. Press the seam allowances toward the medium dark rectangle. Make seven.

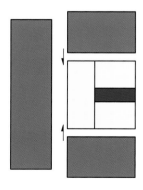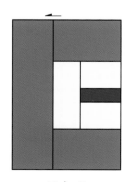

Make 7.

3. Sew medium light 2½" x 4½" rectangles to both the top and bottom of the unit as shown. Press the seam allowances toward the center. Sew a medium light 2½" x 10" rectangle to the left side of the unit. Press the seam allowances toward the medium light rectangle. Make seven.

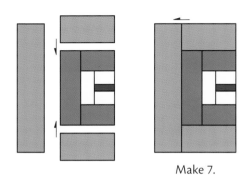

Make 7.

4. To make the A block, sew a dark 3" x 6½" rectangle to the top of the unit, pressing the seam allowances toward the center. Add a dark 3" x 12½" rectangle to the left side of the unit. Press the seam allowances toward the rectangle. Make four A blocks measuring 9" x 12½".

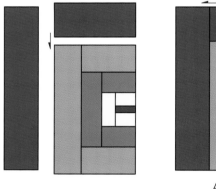

A block.
Make 4.

5. To make the B block, rotate the unit as shown, and sew a dark 3" x 6½" rectangle to the top of the rotated unit. Press the seam allowances toward the center. Sew a dark 3" x 12½" rectangle to the right side of the unit, pressing the seam allowances toward the dark rectangle. Make three B blocks measuring 9" x 12½".

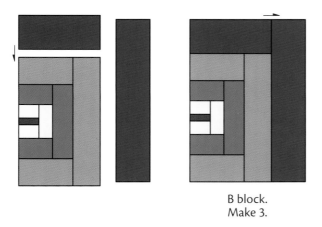

B block.
Make 3.

6. Sew the A and B blocks into a vertical row, starting with an A block and alternating blocks. Press the seam allowances toward the top of the row.

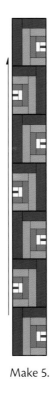

Make 5.

7. Repeat steps 1 through 6 with four other fabric sets to make a total of five vertical A-B rows.

MAKING THE C AND D BLOCK ROWS

1. Use the same combinations of fabrics to make one vertical row of C and D blocks. Follow steps 1 through 3 for the A and B blocks, but alternate the values and press all seam allowances away from the center. Make seven units as shown.

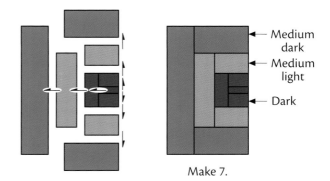

Medium dark
Medium light
Dark

Make 7.

2. To make the C block, rotate the unit as shown and sew a light 3" x 6½" rectangle to the top of the rotated unit. Press the seam allowances away from the center. Sew a light 3" x 12½" rectangle to the right side and press. Make four C blocks.

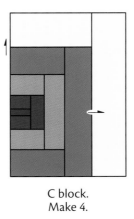

C block.
Make 4.

3. To make the D block, sew a light 3" x 6½" rectangle to the top of the unit and press away from the center. Add a light 3" x 12½" rectangle to the left side of the unit and press. Make three D blocks.

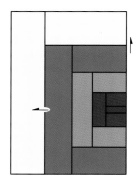

D block.
Make 3.

4. Sew the C and D blocks into a vertical row, starting with a C block and alternating blocks. Press the seam allowances toward the bottom.

5. Repeat steps 1 through 4 with the other three fabric sets to make a total of four C-D rows.

QUILT-TOP ASSEMBLY

Arrange the vertical rows, starting with an A-B row and alternating with the C-D rows until you are happy with the overall look. Sew the rows together, pressing the seam allowances toward the center row.

FINISHING THE QUILT

Refer to "Quiltmaking Basics" on page 76 as needed to complete the following steps.

1. Make a backing 3" to 5" larger on all sides than your quilt top.

2. Layer the quilt top with the batting and backing. Baste the layers together.

3. Quilt by hand or machine using the design of your choice.

4. Square up the quilt.

5. Prepare the binding and sew it to the quilt.

6. Add a label and a hanging sleeve, if desired, to complete your quilt.

QUILTING SUGGESTIONS

This project features a quilting design I call Dragon's Tail. It is a continuous design, but I tend to stop and start for almost every new tail.

STRIPS AND STRIPES

Designed by Ilene Bartos. Pieced and quilted by Penny Lupo, Sierra Vista, Arizona.

Finished Quilt: 75½" x 84½" ▪ Finished Block: 9" x 12"

This quilt combines a variety of simple piecing techniques with beautiful batiks to achieve a wonderfully subtle look. The lights and darks dance around the quilt top, keeping the viewer interested. For a super quick and easy version, replace all the pieced sections with a print fabric and strip piece the whole quilt.

MATERIALS

All yardages are based on 42"-wide fabric.

3⅓ yards *total* of a variety of light/medium batik fabrics for blocks*

3⅓ yards *total* of a variety of medium/dark batik fabrics for blocks*

2⅛ yards of batik print for border and binding

5½ yards of fabric for backing

81" x 90" piece of batting

Colors have different values depending on the colors placed next to them. A medium-value color will look "light" if placed next to darker colors but will look "dark" if placed next to lighter colors. Therefore I am calling the colors "light/medium" and "medium/dark" throughout this project.

CUTTING

Patterns for templates A, B, C, and D are on page 23.

From the light/medium batiks, cut:
- 21 strips, 3½" x 42"; crosscut into:
    - 22 rectangles, 3½" x 12½"
    - 33 rectangles, 3½" x 9½"
    - 27 triangles using pattern A
    - 5 triangles using pattern B
    - 4 triangles using pattern C
    - 4 triangles using pattern D
- 3 strips, 3⅞" x 42"; crosscut into 23 squares, 3⅞" x 3⅞"
- 5 strips, 4¼" x 42"; crosscut into 37 squares, 4¼" x 4¼"

From the medium/dark batiks, cut:
- 21 strips, 3½" x 42"; crosscut into:
    - 22 rectangles, 3½" x 12½"
    - 32 rectangles, 3½" x 9½"
    - 28 triangles using pattern A
    - 5 triangles using pattern B
    - 3 triangles using pattern C
    - 3 triangles using pattern D
- 3 strips, 3⅞" x 42"; crosscut into 23 squares, 3⅞" x 3⅞"
- 5 strips, 4¼" x 42"; crosscut into 37 squares, 4¼" x 4¼"

From the batik print for border and binding, cut:
- 7 strips, 6½" x 42"
- 9 binding strips, 2½" x 42"

MAKING TRIANGLE-SQUARE SECTIONS

1. Place a light/medium 3⅞" square on top of a medium/dark 3⅞" square. Draw a diagonal line on the wrong side of the lighter square and sew ¼" from the line on both sides.

2. Cut on the diagonal line and press the seam allowances toward the darker fabric. Trim points. Repeat to make 46; one is extra.

Make 46.

3. Place four triangle squares side by side, positioning them so that the darker fabrics are on the lower right as shown. Sew together to make a 3½" x 12½" section, pressing the seam allowances in one direction. Make six sections.

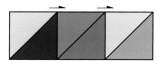

Make 6.

4. Repeat step 3 to sew three triangle squares together to make a 3½" x 9½" section. Make seven sections.

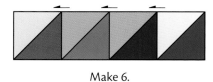

Make 7.

MAKING HOURGLASS SECTIONS

1. Place a light/medium 4¼" square on top of a medium/dark 4¼" square. Draw a line from corner to corner on the wrong side of the lighter square and sew ¼" from the line on both sides. Cut on the diagonal line and press the seam allowances toward the darker fabric. Trim points.

2. Layer the two triangle squares, right sides together, on top of each other, with the dark triangle on top of the light so the seams will snuggle. Draw a line from corner to corner in the opposite direction of the seam and sew ¼" from the line on both sides.

3. Cut on the diagonal line and press the seam allowances to one side. Trim points and repeat to make 74; one is extra.

Make 74.

4. Place four hourglass units side by side, positioning them so that the darks are on the top and bottom. Sew them together to make a 3½" x 12½" section, pressing the seam allowances open or to one side if you prefer. Make five sections. Repeat with three hourglass units per section to make six sections, 3½" x 9½".

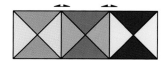

Make 5.

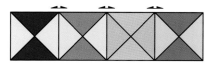

Make 6.

5. Sew four hourglass units together with the lights on the top and bottom to make a 3½" x 12½" section. Sew three hourglass units together with the lights on the top and bottom to make a 3½" x 9½" section. Make five of each.

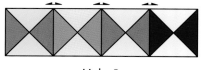

Make 5.

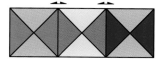

Make 6.

MAKING 60°-TRIANGLE SECTIONS

1. Arrange four A triangles together with two B triangles, positioning darks and lights as shown. Sew together to make a 3½" x 9½" strip. Press the seam allowances to one side and trim points. Make five sections.

Make 5.

2. Arrange five A triangles, one C triangle, and one D triangle together, positioning darks and lights as shown. Sew together to make a 3½" x 12½" strip. Press the seam allowances and trim points. Make four sections with light/medium on the ends and three sections with medium/dark on the ends.

Make 4.

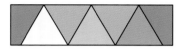

Make 3.

MAKING THE BLOCKS

1. Arrange one pieced 3½" x 12½" triangle-square section between two batik 3½" x 12½" rectangles. Sew together to make a 9½" x 12½" A block. Press the seam allowances toward the unpieced rectangles. Set aside one 12½" triangle-square section and one 12½" 60°-triangle section for the border. Using all the remaining pieced 3½" x 12½" sections, make a total of 21 A blocks.

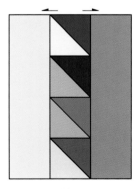

A block.
Make 21.

2. Sew the 3½" x 12½" triangle-square section to a batik rectangle as shown to make an A border unit. Press the seam allowances toward the rectangle. Repeat to sew the 3½" x 12½" 60° triangle section to a batik rectangle to make a second A border block.

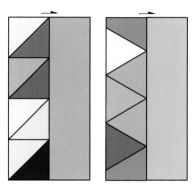

A border blocks

3. Arrange one pieced 3½" x 9½" triangle-square section and three batik 3½" x 9½" rectangles as shown. Sew together to make a 9½" x 12½" B block. Press the seam allowances away from the pieced strip. Set aside one 9½" hourglass section and one triangle-square section for the border. Using all the remaining 3½" x 9½" pieced sections, make a total of 21 B blocks.

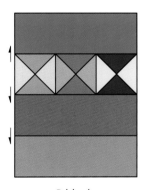

B block.
Make 21.

4. Sew the 3½" x 9½" half-square-triangle section to a batik rectangle as shown to make a B border unit. Repeat with the quarter-square section to make two B border units.

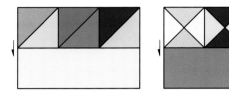

B border blocks

QUILT-TOP ASSEMBLY

1. Arrange the blocks in six rows of seven blocks each, alternating the A and B blocks. Rotate half of the B blocks so that the pieced sections are closer to the top in half and closer to the bottom in the other half. Refer to the quilt layout as needed.

COLOR BALANCE

Make sure to balance the colors throughout the quilt top before sewing. Bright colors have more weight than soft colors and should be spaced evenly throughout the top.

2. Sew the blocks together in rows, pressing the seam allowances in the opposite direction from row to row.

3. Sew the rows together to complete the center. The quilt top should measure 63½" x 72½".

ADDING THE BORDERS

If your quilt top doesn't measure 63½" x 72½", you will need to adjust the border strips before cutting, lengthening or shortening them as needed. The seams of the border units should match the seams of the blocks.

1. Piece and cut the 6½" border strips as follows.
   Right border: 6½" x 24½" and 6½" x 36½"
   Left border: 6½" x 12½" and 6½" x 48½"
   Top border: 6½" x 24½" and 6½" x 42½"
   Bottom border: 6½" x 15½" and 6½" x 51½"

2. For the right border, refer to the quilt diagram to sew an A border block between the two right border strips. Press the seam allowances away from the pieced block. Repeat for the left side, using the left border pieces and an A border block. Sew the borders to the side edges of the quilt top, pressing the seam allowances toward the borders. Note that the position of the border blocks differs from the quilt shown. Audition both ways to see which you prefer.

3. Sew a B border block between the top border strips; press. Repeat for the bottom, using the bottom border pieces and the last B border block. Sew the borders to the top and bottom edges of the quilt.

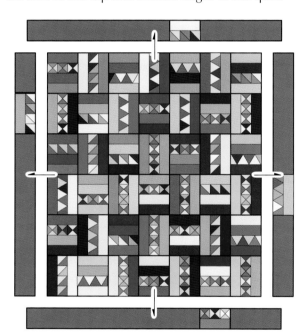

FINISHING THE QUILT

Refer to "Quiltmaking Basics" on page 76 as needed to complete the following steps.

1. Make a backing 3" to 5" larger on all sides than your quilt top.

2. Layer the quilt top with the batting and backing. Baste the layers together.

3. Quilt by hand or machine using the design of your choice. Square up the quilt.

4. Prepare the binding and sew it to the quilt.

5. Add a label and a hanging sleeve, if desired, to complete your quilt.

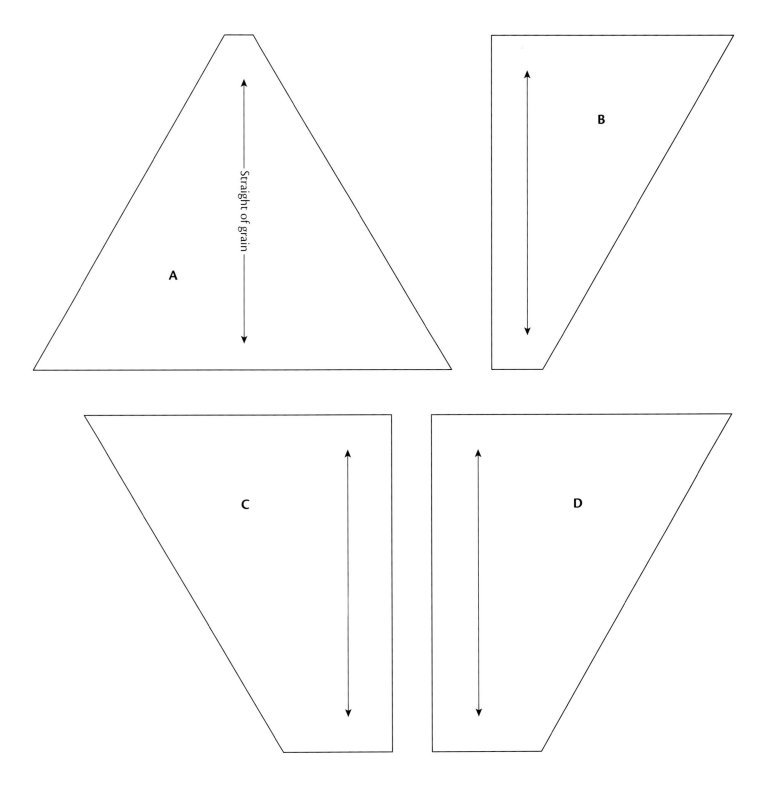

A

Straight of grain

B

C

D

BLAZE OF GOLD

Designed and quilted by Ilene Bartos. Pieced by Marie Zupan, Omaha, Nebraska.
Finished Quilt: 94½" x 94½" ▪ Finished Block: 8" x 10"

Log Cabin blocks are usually made up of rectangular strips sewn around a square to form a square block. Because I wanted to make a rectangular block, I started with a rectangle in the center. The result is a dynamic block arranged in an exciting, offset design that looks like a touch of lightning. I used blacks and golds with a touch of metallic sparkle for my version of this easy-to-sew quilt.

MATERIALS

All yardages are based on 42"-wide fabric.

5 yards *total* of a variety of black prints for blocks

3⅝ yards *total* of a variety of gold prints for blocks

2⅛ yards of gold paisley print for block centers and outer border

1⅛ yards of solid black fabric for block centers and binding

½ yard of black print for inner border

9⅝ yards of fabric for backing

101" x 101" piece of batting

CUTTING

From the solid black fabric, cut:
- 4 strips, 2½" x 42"
- 10 binding strips, 2½" x 42"

From the gold paisley print, cut:
- 4 strips, 2½" x 42"
- 9 strips, 6½" x 42"

From the black prints, cut a total of:
- 80 rectangles, 1½" x 3½"
- 80 rectangles, 1½" x 4½"
- 80 rectangles, 1½" x 5½"
- 80 rectangles, 1½" x 6½"
- 80 rectangles, 1½" x 7½"
- 80 rectangles, 1½" x 8½"
- 80 rectangles, 1½" x 10½"

From the gold prints, cut a total of:
- 80 rectangles, 1½" x 2½"
- 80 rectangles, 1½" x 4½"
- 80 rectangles, 1½" x 5½"
- 80 rectangles, 1½" x 6½"
- 80 rectangles, 1½" x 7½"
- 80 rectangles, 1½" x 9½"

From the black print for inner border, cut:
- 9 strips, 1½" x 42"

MAKING THE BLOCKS

1. Sew a solid black 2½" strip and a gold paisley 2½" strip together to make a strip set. Press the seam allowances toward the black fabric. Make four strip sets. Crosscut into 80 rectangles, 1½" wide.

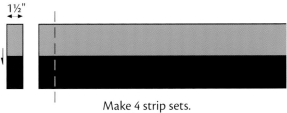

1½"

Make 4 strip sets.
Cut 80 segments.

2. Rotate a rectangle from step 1 so that the black is on the bottom and sew a black print 1½" x 4½" rectangle to the right side as shown. Press the seam allowances toward the black rectangle. Make 80.

3. Follow the diagram below for sewing order and correct placement. Sew a gold 1½" x 2½" rectangle to the top of the unit. Press the seam allowances away from the center.

4. Sew a gold 1½" x 5" rectangle to the left side; press the seam allowances away from the center. Continue adding rectangles in a counterclockwise manner until you've added the black print 1½" x 10½" rectangle. The block should measure 8½" x 10½". Make 80 blocks.

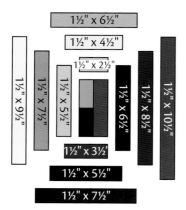

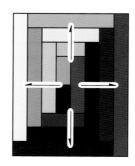

Make 80.

QUILT-TOP ASSEMBLY

1. Arrange the blocks in four rows of five blocks each, following the diagram for rotation of each block.

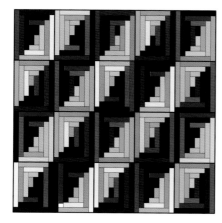

Make 4.

2. Sew the blocks in each row together, pressing in the opposite direction in alternate rows. Sew the rows together to complete one quarter of the quilt top; this section should measure 40½" x 40½". Make four sections.

3. Lay out all four sections, rotating them as shown. Sew the four sections together to complete the quilt top. The top should now measure 80½" x 80½".

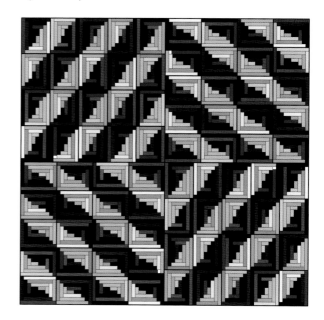

ADDING THE BORDERS

1. Refer to "Measuring Borders" on page 75. Piece and cut two 1½"-wide inner-border strips and sew them to the side edges of the quilt. Press the seam allowances toward the border strips. Repeat to add the inner-border strips to the top and bottom edges.

2. Measure, piece, and cut the 6½"-wide gold paisley outer-border strips, and sew them to the side edges of the quilt top. Press the seam allowances toward the outer border. Repeat for the top and bottom borders.

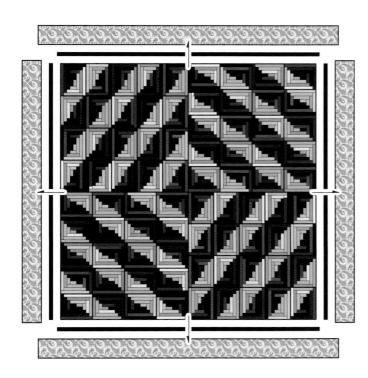

FINISHING THE QUILT

Refer to "Quiltmaking Basics" on page 76 as needed to complete the following steps.

1. Make a backing 3" to 5" larger on all sides than your quilt top.

2. Layer the quilt top with the batting and backing. Baste the layers together.

3. Quilt by hand or machine using the design of your choice.

4. Square up the quilt.

5. Prepare the binding and sew it to the quilt.

6. Add a label and a hanging sleeve, if desired, to complete your quilt.

QUILTING SUGGESTION

The curvy spine of the quilting design I call Ferns adds depth and motion to this quilt.

RINGS AND THINGS

*Designed by Ilene Bartos. Pieced by Sandy Hempfling and
quilted by Sally Morge, both of Las Cruces, New Mexico.*

Finished Quilt: 43½" x 55½" ▪ Finished Block: 12" x 20"

This lap quilt of cozy blue and green flannels is the perfect size to cuddle up under. You could also make it as a quick and easy baby quilt. The two-color design is simple, but using a variety of fabrics in each color provides interest. You can use any colors you want, so pick a wonderful print for the border and have fun!

MATERIALS

All yardages are based on 42"-wide fabric.

1 yard of teal print for outer border and binding

⅛ yard *each* of 6 coordinating blue prints

⅓ yard *each* of 2 solid blue fabrics for rings

⅓ yard *each* of 2 solid green fabrics for rings

⅛ yard *each* of 4 coordinating green prints

⅝ yard of dark blue fabric for inner border

3⅛ yards of fabric for backing

49" x 61" piece of batting

CUTTING

From each of the 2 solid blue and 2 solid green fabrics, cut:
- 2 strips, 4½" x 42"; crosscut into 4 rectangles, 4½" x 12½" (16 total)

From each of the 6 coordinating blue prints, cut:
- 1 strip, 2½" x 42"; crosscut into 8 rectangles, 2½" x 4½" (48 total)

From each of the 4 coordinating green prints, cut:
- 1 strip, 2½" x 42"; crosscut into 8 rectangles, 2½" x 4½" (32 total)

From the dark blue inner-border fabric, cut:
- 5 strips, 3½" x 42"

From the teal print, cut:
- 5 strips, 3" x 42"
- 6 binding strips, 2½" x 42"

MAKING THE RING BLOCKS

1. Sew two different blue 2½" x 4½" rectangles together as shown to make a 4½" square unit. Press the seam allowances to either side. Sew two coordinating green 2½" x 4½" rectangles in the same manner. Make 24 blue units and 16 green units.

Make 24.   Make 16.

2. Sew three blue units from step 1 together, rotating them as shown to make a 4½" x 12½" section. Press the seam allowances toward the center unit. Sew three green units together in the same manner. Make four blue sections and two green sections.

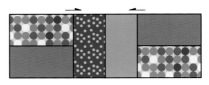

Make 4.

Make 2.

3. Sew solid green 4½" x 12½" rectangles to opposite sides of a blue pieced section from step 2. Press the seam allowances toward the rectangles. Sew solid green 4½" x 12½" rectangles to both the top and bottom to complete the Ring block. Press the seam allowances toward the rectangles. Make two.

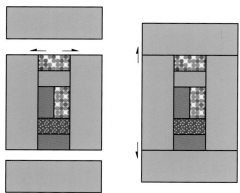

Make 2.

4. Repeat step 3 to sew the solid blue 4½" x 12½" rectangles and green pieced sections together. Make two.

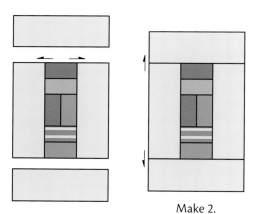

Make 2.

5. Sew six blue square units together, rotating them as shown. Press the seam allowances as indicated by the arrows. Make two.

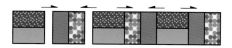

Make 2.

6. Sew five green square units together, rotating them as shown, and press. Make two.

Make 2.

QUILT-TOP ASSEMBLY

1. Sew a green section from step 6 of "Making the Ring Blocks" to the right side of a blue Ring block. Press the seam allowances toward the ring. Make two.

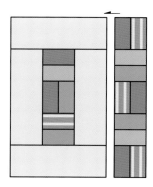

Make 2.

2. Sew a blue section from step 2 to the top of a green Ring block. Press the seam allowances toward the ring. Sew a blue section from step 5 to the left side of the green Ring block. Press the seam allowances toward the ring. Make two.

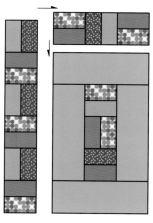

Make 2.

3. Arrange the block units in two vertical rows of two units each, rotating them as shown. Sew the units together in rows and press. Sew the rows together, and press the seam allowances in either direction. The quilt top should now measure 32½" x 44½".

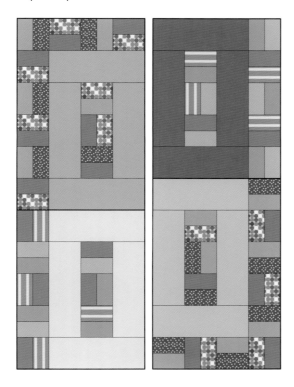

4. Refer to "Measuring Borders" on page 75. Measure, piece, and cut two 3½"-wide inner-border strips and sew them to the side edges of the quilt top. Press the seam allowances toward the borders. Repeat for the top and bottom inner-border strips.

5. Measure, piece, and cut two 3"-wide outer-border strips and sew them to the side edges of the quilt. Press the seam allowances toward the borders.

Repeat for the top and bottom outer-border strips. Press the seam allowances toward the borders.

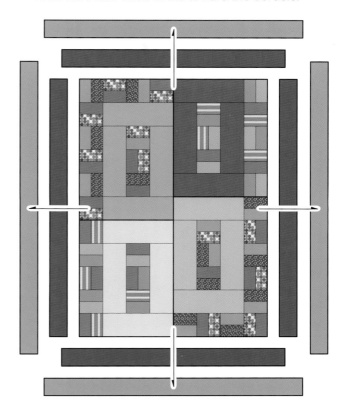

FINISHING THE QUILT

Refer to "Quiltmaking Basics" on page 76 as needed to complete the following steps.

1. Make a backing 3" to 5" larger on all sides than your quilt top.

2. Layer the quilt top with the batting and backing. Baste the layers together.

3. Quilt by hand or machine using the design of your choice.

4. Square up the quilt.

5. Prepare the binding and sew it to the quilt.

6. Add a label and a hanging sleeve, if desired.

QUILTING SUGGESTION

The rings are quilted with straight lines around the rectangles; two circles are quilted in each small rectangle. The borders are quilted with a gentle swirling design.

CHAINS OF HOPE

Designed and quilted by Ilene Bartos. Pieced by Shelley Mitchell of Des Moines, Iowa.
Finished Quilt: 60½" x 69½" ▪ Finished Block: 3" x 12"

One of my favorite color combinations is blacks and whites with brights; the colors play off each other and create dynamic, sparkling quilts. This colorful quilt is a good example, using a rainbow of bright fabrics "chained" together with blacks and whites. Use up your bright scraps on this fun project when you need a dose of hope, or when a special someone could use a colorful gift of encouragement.

MATERIALS

All yardages are based on 42"-wide fabric.

1⅝ yards of dotted black print for border

1¼ yards *total* of black prints for "chains"

1¼ yards *total* of white prints for "chains"

⅔ yard *total* of blue prints for blocks

⅝ yard *total* of teal prints for blocks

⅝ yard *total* of purple prints for blocks

½ yard *total* of green prints for blocks

½ yard *total* of red prints for blocks

¼ yard *total* of yellow prints for blocks

¼ yard *total* of orange prints for blocks

¼ yard *total* of lime green prints for blocks

⅝ yard of solid black fabric for binding

4 yards of fabric for backing

67" x 76" piece of batting

Template plastic or Quarter Circle Template Set (see "Resources" on page 79)

CUTTING

From the yellow prints, cut:
- 2 rectangles, 3½" x 9½"
- 2 rectangles, 3½" x 6½"
- 2 squares, 3½" x 3½"

From the orange prints, cut:
- 4 rectangles, 3½" x 12½"
- 1 rectangle, 3½" x 9½"
- 1 rectangle, 3½" x 6½"
- 1 square, 3½" x 3½"

From the red prints, cut:
- 8 rectangles, 3½" x 12½"
- 1 rectangle, 3½" x 9½"
- 1 rectangle, 3½" x 6½"
- 1 square, 3½" x 3½"

From the purple prints, cut:
- 12 rectangles, 3½" x 12½"
- 1 rectangle, 3½" x 9½"
- 1 rectangle, 3½" x 6½"
- 1 square, 3½" x 3½"

From the blue prints, cut:
- 13 rectangles, 3½" x 12½"
- 2 rectangles, 3½" x 9½"
- 2 rectangles, 3½" x 6½"
- 2 squares, 3½" x 3½"

From the teal prints, cut:
- 12 rectangles, 3½" x 12½"
- 1 rectangle, 3½" x 9½"
- 1 rectangle, 3½" x 6½"
- 1 square, 3½" x 3½"

From the green prints, cut:

- 8 rectangles, 3½" x 12½"
- 1 rectangle, 3½" x 9½"
- 1 rectangle, 3½ x 6½"
- 1 square, 3½" x 3½"

From the lime green prints, cut:

- 4 rectangles, 3½" x 12½"
- 1 rectangle, 3½" x 9½"
- 1 rectangle, 3½" x 6½"
- 1 square, 3½" x 3½"

From the dotted black print, cut:

- 9 strips, 3½" x 42"; crosscut into:
    16 rectangles, 3½" x 12½"
    2 rectangles, 3½" x 9½"
    2 rectangles, 3½" x 6½"
    22 squares, 3½" x 3½"
- 3 strips, 6½" x 42"; crosscut into 10 rectangles, 6½" x 9½"

From the black prints, cut:

- 11 strips, 3½" by 42"; crosscut into 115 squares, 3½" x 3½"

From the white prints, cut:

- 11 strips, 3½" x 42"; crosscut into 115 squares, 3½" x 3½".

From the solid black fabric, cut:

- 7 strips, 2½" x 42"

CUTTING THE QUARTER CIRCLES

1. Make a template from template plastic using the background pattern on page 37, or use a purchased Background Ruler from the Quarter Circle Template Set. Cut two quarter circles from each 12½" rectangle, rotating them as shown. Discard the quarter circles or use the scraps in another project.

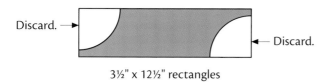

3½" x 12½" rectangles

2. Cut one quarter circle from each of the 3½" x 9½" and 3½" x 6½" rectangles and 3½" squares as shown. Discard the quarter circles. Do not cut the black or white print 3½" squares.

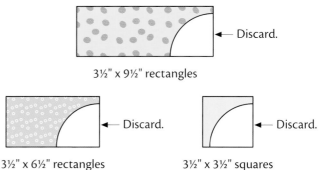

3½" x 9½" rectangles

3½" x 6½" rectangles   3½" x 3½" squares

3. Cut two quarter circles from the dotted black 6½" x 9½" rectangles for the border, rotating them as shown.

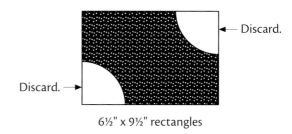

6½" x 9½" rectangles

4. Make a template using the inset template pattern on page 37, or use the Inset Ruler from the Quarter Circle Template Set. Cut a quarter circle from each of the black print 3½" squares. Discard the outer sliver of fabric. Repeat for the white print 3½" squares.

MAKING THE BLOCKS

1. Sew one black quarter circle and one white quarter circle to each end of a 3½" x 12½" rectangle. Press seam allowances on the black circles toward the rectangle and seam allowances on the white circles toward the circles. Repeat for all 77 rectangles.

Make 77.

SEWING CURVED SEAMS

1. Finger-press to find the center of both the inset and the background curve. Pin the centers together.

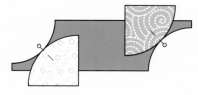

2. With the inset on the top, begin at the corner to align the edges so the side of the inset is even with the top of the rectangle. Place a pin at the end and sew to the center pin, keeping the raw edges aligned and even so that you will have an accurate ¼" seam allowance. To help you get a grip, use a pair of tweezers to hold the edges even while sewing curves.

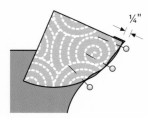

3. At the center, leave the needle down in the fabric and lift the presser foot, removing the pin. Adjust the ends of the fabric so that the corner of the inset is aligned with the bottom of the rectangle and pin together. Sew the rest of the seam, adjusting often to keep the raw edges even.

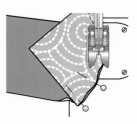

2. Referring to the diagram, sew either a white or black quarter circle to each of the 3½" x 9½" rectangles, 3½" x 6½" rectangles, and 3½" squares. Press seam allowances on the black circles toward the rectangle or square and seam allowances on the white circles toward the circles.

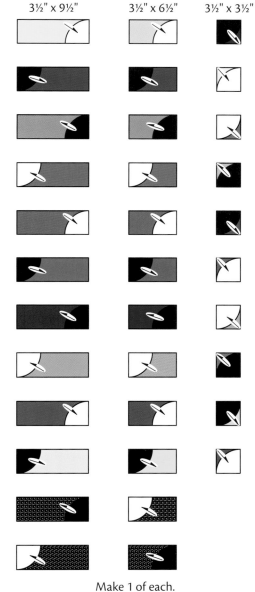

Make 1 of each.

Make 11 of each.

3. Sew a white inset to one corner and a black inset to the opposite corner of the 6½" x 9½" black dotted rectangles cut previously. Make 10.

Make 10.

QUILT-TOP ASSEMBLY

1. Referring to the quilt diagram as needed, lay out the rectangles and squares in rows, making sure you are pleased with the color arrangement.

2. Sew the pieces in each row together, making vertical rows for the side borders as shown. Press seam allowances in alternate directions from row to row. Sew the rows together to complete the quilt top, adding the top and bottom rows last. The quilt top should measure 60½" x 69½".

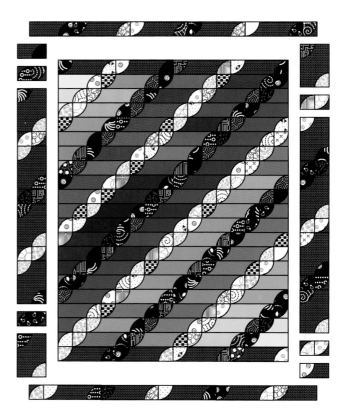

FINISHING THE QUILT

Refer to "Quiltmaking Basics" on page 76 as needed to complete the following steps.

1. Make a backing 3" to 5" larger on all sides than your quilt top.

2. Layer the quilt top with the batting and backing. Baste the layers together.

3. Quilt by hand or machine using the design of your choice.

4. Square up the quilt.

5. Prepare the binding and sew it to the quilt.

6. Add a label and a hanging sleeve, if desired, to complete your quilt.

QUILTING SUGGESTION

This quilt is quilted with variegated thread in a simple overall flower design.

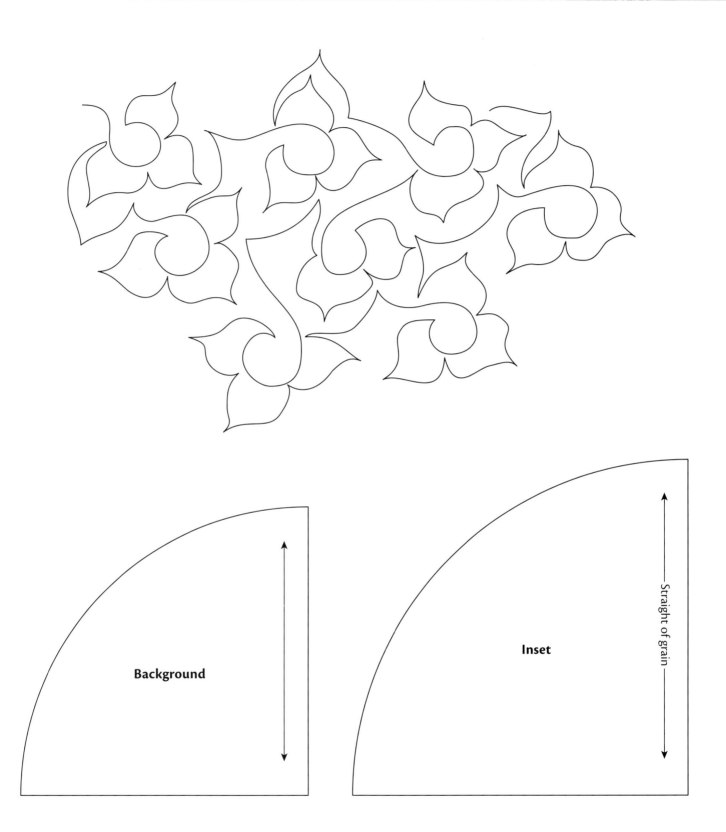

Background

Inset

Straight of grain

JUNGLE MAZE

Designed and made by Ilene Bartos.

Finished Quilt: 80½" x 98½" ▪ Finished Block: 8" x 10"

A collection of blue, green, and teal batik fabrics made this a perfect quilt for my daughter, Nikki, as those are her favorite colors. All the greens make me feel like I'm in the middle of a tropical jungle, while the splashes of orange remind me of colorful flowers or birds. The rectangular blocks are arranged in both directions, but don't worry about set-in seams—the blocks are sewn together with numerous partial seams.

MATERIALS

All yardages are based on 42"-wide fabric.

½ yard *each* of 14 assorted blue, green, and teal fabrics for blocks

½ yard *each* of 4 orange fabrics for block centers

1½ yards of green fabric for block centers

⅞ yard of fabric for binding

7½ yards of fabric for backing

87" x 105" piece of batting

CUTTING

From the green fabric for block centers, cut:
- 11 strips, 3½" x 42"
- 1 strip, 2½" x 42"

From the orange fabrics for block centers, cut a total of:
- 11 strips, 3½" x 42"
- 1 strip, 2½" x 42"
- 4 strips, 2⅞" x 42"

From the assorted blue, green, and teal fabrics, cut a total of:
- 82 strips, 2½" x 42"; crosscut into:
    - 384 rectangles, 2½" x 4½"
    - 352 rectangles, 2½" x 3½"
    - 32 squares, 2½" x 2½"
- 4 strips, 2⅞" x 42"

From the binding fabric, cut:
- 10 strips, 2½" x 42"

MAKING THE BLOCK CENTERS

1. Sew a 3½" x 42" green strip and a 3½" x 42" orange strip together to make a strip set. Press the seam allowances toward the green fabric. Repeat to make 11 strip sets total. Crosscut the strip sets every 2½" to make 176 segments, 2½" x 6½".

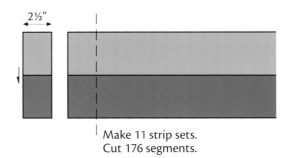

2½"

Make 11 strip sets.
Cut 176 segments.

2. Sew the 2½" x 42" green strip and the 2½" x 42" orange strip together to make a strip set. Press the seam allowances toward the green fabric. Cross-cut the strip set every 2½" to make 16 segments, 2½" x 4½".

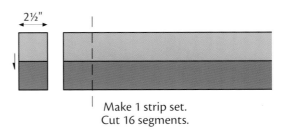

2½"

Make 1 strip set.
Cut 16 segments.

3. Sew together two of the 2½" x 6½" segments from step 1, rotating one as shown. Press the seam allowances to one side. Repeat to make 84 center units, 4½" x 6½". Set aside eight extra segments to be used later in the C blocks.

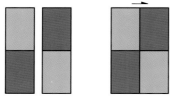

Make 84.

4. Sew together two of the 2½" x 4½" segments from step 2, rotating one as shown. Press the seam allowances to one side. Repeat to make four center units, 4½" x 4½". Set aside eight extra segments to be used later in the D blocks.

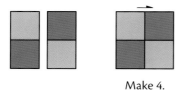

Make 4.

MAKING THE A BLOCKS

1. Select two different green, blue, or teal fabrics and use two 2½" x 3½" rectangles and two 2½" x 4½" rectangles of each. Arrange them around a 4½" x 6½" center unit as shown, placing matching fabrics in the corners.

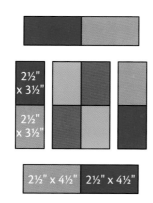

2. Sew the outer rectangles together in pairs along the short ends. Press the seam allowances in the opposite direction of the center unit. Sew the shorter rectangle units to the sides of the center. Press the seam allowances away from the center. Sew the longer rectangle units to the top and bottom to complete the A block. Press the seam allowances away from the center. The block should measure 8½" x 10½". Repeat to make 84.

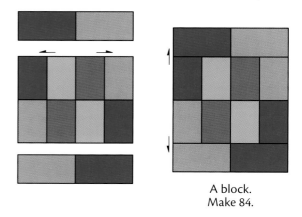

A block.
Make 84.

MAKING THE B BLOCKS

1. Select two different green, blue, or teal fabrics and use two 2½" squares and two 2½" x 4½" rectangles of each. Arrange them around a 4½" x 4½" center unit, placing matching fabrics in the corners.

2. Sew the squares together and press the seam allowances in the opposite direction of the center unit. Sew the rectangles together on the short ends; press the seam allowances in the opposite direction of the center unit. Sew the square units to each side of the center unit and the rectangle units to the top and bottom. Press the seam allowances away from the center. The B block should measure 8½" x 8½". Repeat to make four.

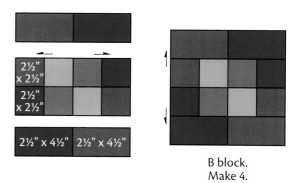

B block.
Make 4.

MAKING THE C BLOCKS

1. Select two different green, blue, or teal fabrics and use one 2½" x 3½" rectangle and one 2½" x 4½" rectangle from each. Arrange them around a reserved 2½" x 6½" center segment, placing matching fabrics in the corners.

2. Sew the 2½" x 3½" rectangles together on the short ends and press the seam allowances in the opposite direction of the center segment. Sew this unit to the right side of the segment, pressing the seam allowances away from the center. Sew the 2½" x 4½" rectangles to both the top and bottom to complete the 4½" x 10½" C block. Press the seam allowances away from the center. Repeat to make eight.

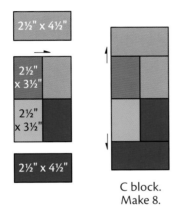

C block.
Make 8.

MAKING THE D BLOCKS

1. Select two different green, blue, or teal fabrics and use one 2½" square and one 2½" x 4½" rectangle from each. Arrange them around a reserved 2½" x 4½" center segment, placing matching fabrics in the corners.

2. Sew the squares together and press the seam allowances in the opposite direction of the center segment. Sew this unit to one side of the center segment. Press the seam allowances away from the center. Sew a rectangle to the top and bottom to complete

the 4½" x 8½" D block. Press the seam allowances away from the center. Repeat to make eight.

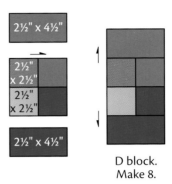

D block.
Make 8.

MAKING THE E BLOCKS

1. Layer a 2⅞" strip of green, blue, or teal and a 2⅞" orange strip right sides together, and cut nine pairs of 2⅞" squares. Cut each of the layered squares in half once diagonally to make 18 pairs of triangles.

Cut.

2. Sew the triangles together along the bias edges, being careful not to stretch the fabric. Press the seam allowances toward the darker color and trim the points. Make 18 matching triangle squares.

Sew.   Make 18.

3. Arrange nine triangle squares in a row, making sure to rotate the blocks as shown. Sew them together to create a unit 2½" x 18½". Make two units, and then repeat with the remaining 2⅞" strips to make a total of eight E blocks.

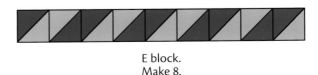

E block.
Make 8.

QUILT-TOP ASSEMBLY

1. Select two A blocks and position as shown. Sew together, leaving 2" unsewn in a partial seam. Refer to "Partial Seams" on page 72 for details. Repeat to make 34.

2. Arrange the block units from step 1 and the remaining blocks together as shown into two matching halves for the top and bottom. Make sure the color arrangement is balanced and pleasing to you before sewing them together.

Leave 2" unsewn.

Make 34.

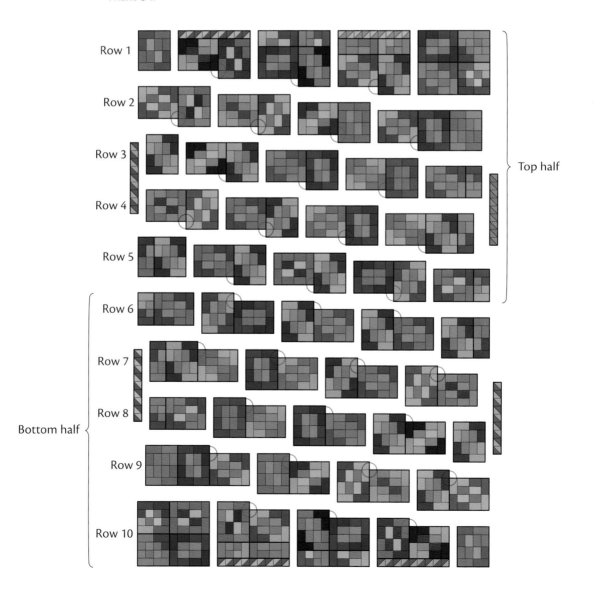

3. Sew the blocks together into units as shown. There will be four E blocks not yet attached to any other blocks. Sew the row 1 units together, joining the vertical seams first. Repeat for the first five rows, leaving partial seams where necessary.

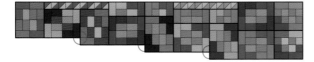

Sew Row 1 vertical seams.

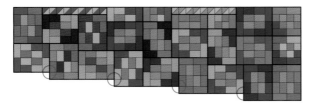

Sew horizontal seams of Row 2 sections to Row 1.
Sew partial (vertical) seams.

4. Sew row 1 and row 2 together, beginning with the horizontal seams. Sew the partial vertical seams next. There will still be partial sections along the bottom of row 2 that will be needed when attaching row 3.

5. Sew row 3 and row 4 together, and then finish the partial seams of row 3. Sew an E block to each end of the row.

6. Sew rows 3-4 to rows 1-2 and then finish the partial seams of row 2.

7. Sew row 5 to the top and then finish the partial seams of row 4.

8. Begin with row 10, and sew pairs of rows together in the same manner to create the bottom half of the quilt. Join the rows, finishing partial seams as you go to complete the bottom half of the quilt top. Then sew the halves together.

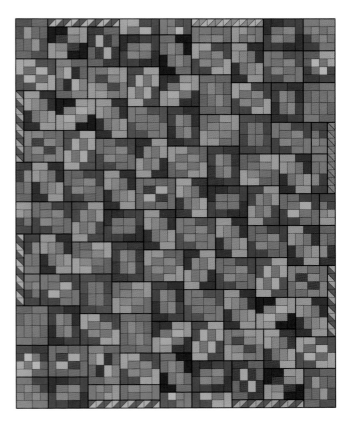

FINISHING THE QUILT

Refer to "Quiltmaking Basics" on page 76 as needed to complete the following steps.

1. Make a backing 3" to 5" larger on all sides than your quilt top.

2. Layer the quilt top with the batting and backing. Baste the layers together.

3. Quilt by hand or machine using the design of your choice.

4. Square up the quilt.

5. Prepare the binding and sew it to the quilt.

6. Add a label and a hanging sleeve, if desired, to complete your quilt.

QUILTING SUGGESTION

This quilt was quilted with variegated thread in a design I call Ferns, shown on page 27.

HOT FLASH

Designed and made by Ilene Bartos.
Finished Quilt: 65" x 88½" ▪ Finished Block: 10½" x 13"

This dynamite quilt is full of bright color and has an added punch because of the contrast between the solids, stripes, and patterned batik. Pick your favorite batik, grab your stripes and bright solids, and have a blast with your stash of fabrics!

MATERIALS

All yardages are based on 42"-wide fabric.

3¼ yards *total* of at least 16 solid fabrics in lights to darks for blocks and pieced border

2⅛ yards of batik for blocks and flat-fold piping

2 yards of taupe solid fabric for setting squares, inner and outer border, and binding

1½ yards *total* of a variety of striped fabrics for blocks

6 yards of fabric for backing

71" x 95" piece of batting

CUTTING

For the blocks, I found it easiest to choose a striped fabric first, and then decide which two solids went best with it. Because the batik has so many different colors in it, they all blend in together and there is no need to match the colors perfectly. For unity, I always put the darkest solid in the center of the block.

For One Block (Make 24 total.)
From a dark solid fabric, cut:
- 1 rectangle, 2" x 4½"

From a medium to light solid fabric, cut:
- 2 rectangles, 2" x 4½"
- 2 rectangles, 2" x 5"

From a striped fabric, cut:
- 2 rectangles, 2" x 7½"
- 2 rectangles, 2" x 8"

For the Remainder of the Quilt
From the batik, cut:
- 48 rectangles, 2" x 10½"
- 48 rectangles, 2" x 11"
- 8 strips, ¾" x 42"

From the taupe solid fabric, cut:
- 1 strip, 3" x 42"; crosscut into 6 squares, 3" x 3"
- 7 strips, 2" x 42"
- 8 strips, 3½" x 42"
- 8 strips, 2½" x 42"

*From **each** of the 16 solid fabrics, cut:*
- 8 to 10 rectangles, 2" x 9" (There will be extra.)

MAKING THE BLOCKS

I found it best to sew each block individually or two at a time to keep from mixing up my colors. The instructions are written for sewing one block at a time.

1. On each side of the dark solid 2" x 4½" rectangle, sew one coordinating solid 2" x 4½" rectangle. Press the seam allowances toward the center. Sew one matching solid 2" x 5" rectangle to the top of the unit and one to the bottom as shown. Press the seam allowances outward.

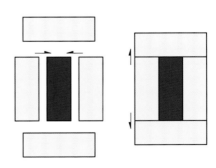

2. To add the next round, sew one striped 2" x 7½" rectangle to each side of the unit from step 1. Press the seam allowances toward the striped rectangle. Sew striped 2" x 8" rectangles to the top and bottom edges as shown. Press the seam allowances outward.

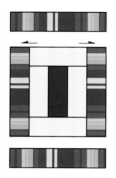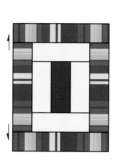

3. Sew a batik 2" x 10½" rectangle to each side of the block. Press the seam allowances toward the batik rectangle. Sew batik 2" x 11" rectangles to the top and bottom edges as shown. Press.

4. Repeat steps 1 to 3 to make 24 blocks measuring 11" x 13½".

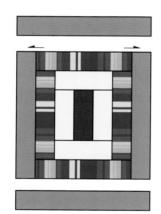

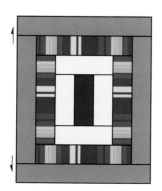

Make 24.

MAKING THE FOUR-BLOCK UNITS

1. Arrange four blocks around one taupe solid 3" square as shown. Two blocks will be horizontal and two blocks will be vertical.

2. Sew the 3" square to block 1 with a partial seam, referring to "Partial Seams" on page 72 as needed. Press only the sewn area toward the block.

3. Sew block 2 to the first unit, pressing the seam allowances toward block 2. In the same manner, sew block 3 to the unit, and then add block 4. Finish the large unit by sewing block 4 to block 1, which will complete the partial seam. Press the seam allowances toward block 1. Repeat to make six large blocks measuring 24" x 24".

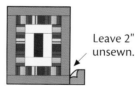

Leave 2" unsewn.

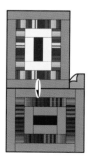

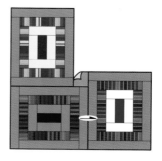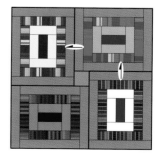

Make 6.

QUILT-TOP ASSEMBLY

1. Place the four-block units in three rows of two blocks each, making sure the colors are pleasing and look balanced to you.

2. Sew each row together, pressing seam allowances in opposite directions from row to row. Sew the rows together to complete the top, which should measure 47½" x 71".

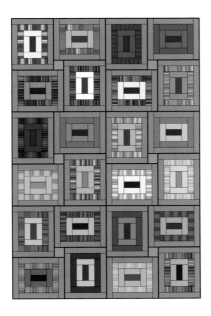

ADDING THE INNER BORDER

1. Refer to "Measuring Borders" on page 75. Measure, piece, and cut two taupe solid 2"-wide inner-border strips and sew them to opposite sides of the quilt top. Press the seam allowances toward the border strips.

2. Measure, piece, and cut two taupe solid 2"-wide inner-border strips for the top and bottom edges. Sew them to the quilt top, and press the seam allowances toward the border strips. The top should now measure 50½" x 74".

MAKING THE PIECED BORDER

1. For the side borders, choose 18 of the solid 2" x 9" rectangles and arrange them from dark to light. Arrange four matching sets.

2. Sew the strips together from dark to light, offsetting each strip by 1¾" as shown. Press seam allowances

toward the darker fabric. You will need two strip sets that are offset to the right and two that are offset to the left.

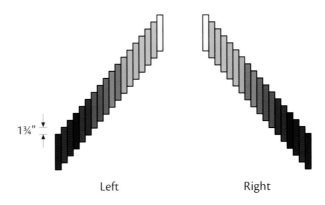

Left   Right

3. For the top and bottom borders, choose 13 of the solid 2" x 9" rectangles and arrange them from dark to light. Make sure not to use the same darkest color that you used for the side borders. Make four matching sets.

4. Sew the strips together from dark to light, offsetting each strip by 1¾". Press the seam allowances toward the darker fabric. Make two left strip sets and two right strip sets.

5. Carefully trim off and discard the points on each of the strips sets as shown. Make sure the sides are exactly parallel to each other; the strip sets should be approximately 4¾" wide. It's more important that all the sets are the same width, so trim them if needed to the size that works best for your strips.

Cut.
Cut.
4¾"

BORDER CONTROL

To help control the bias edges, use heavy-duty spray starch when pressing the pieced border units prior to trimming them. Also, pin carefully and avoid stretching when sewing the border strips onto the quilt top. It will help to sew with the bias edges on the bottom, next to the sewing machine.

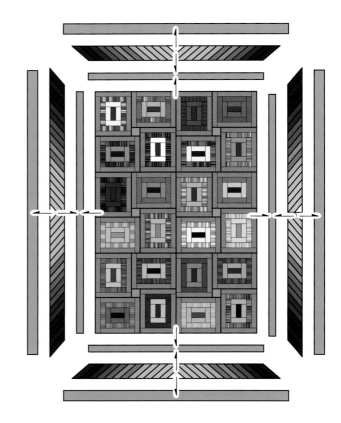

6. Arrange the eight strip sets around your quilt top, making sure they are rotated correctly. Refer to the quilt diagram at right as necessary.

7. Measure your quilt top through the center from top to bottom, divide by two, and add ¼" for the center seam allowance. In a perfect world this will be 37¼".

8. Measure each of the four side border strip sets along the edge that will be sewn to the quilt, not the outside edge of the strip set. Trim off the light end of the strips so that the strips measure the same as determined in step 7. *Don't* cut off the dark end of the strips.

9. Re-press the seam allowances on one of the edges you just cut, so that you will have opposing seam allowances. Sew the two sections of the side border together along the cut edge, matching seams. Press seam allowances open. Repeat to make two side borders.

10. Sew the side borders to the quilt top, beginning and ending ¼" from both the top and bottom of the seam and backstitching at both ends. This will allow you to sew the top and bottom borders together in a mitered seam.

11. Repeat steps 7 through 10 for the top and bottom border strips, measuring the width through the center, from seam to seam; this time, add ¾" to that measurement. Each strip would be 25¾" if all seam allowances are exact.

12. To sew the miter in each corner, align the raw edges of the pieced borders, and pin. Begin sewing ¼" from the corner of the quilt, backstitching to secure the seam. Sew to the outer corner of the border and press the seam allowances open. Sew all corners in the same manner.

ADDING THE OUTER BORDER

1. Measure, piece, and cut two taupe solid 3½"-wide border strips, and sew them to opposite sides of the quilt top. Press the seam allowances toward the borders.

2. Measure, piece, and cut two taupe solid 3½"-wide border strips for the top and bottom edges, and sew them to the quilt top. Press the seam allowances toward the border.

FINISHING THE QUILT

Refer to "Quiltmaking Basics" on page 76 as needed to complete the following steps.

1. Make a backing 3" to 5" larger on all sides than your quilt top.

2. Layer the quilt top with the batting and backing. Baste the layers together.

3. Quilt by hand or machine using the design of your choice.

4. Square up the quilt.

5. Prepare the flat-fold piping, referring to page 74 as needed, and the binding; sew them to the quilt.

6. Add a label and a hanging sleeve, if desired, to complete your quilt.

QUILTING SUGGESTION

Using a variegated thread for the quilting pulls all the colors together. For this design, first stitch a curvy spine and then add curls and swirls all along the spine, starting a new spine in whatever direction is needed next.

BASKET WEAVE

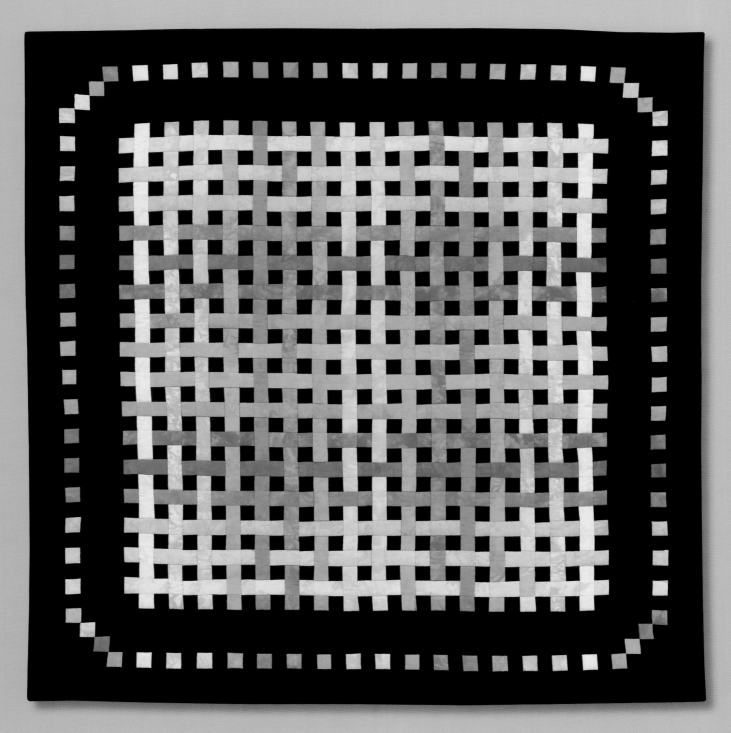

Designed and made by Ilene Bartos.

Finished Quilt: 45½" x 45½" ▪ Finished Block: 3" x 3"

I combined a fat-quarter collection of gradated batiks with a black background to make them really pop. The pieces for this quilt are fairly small, which makes it a bit more challenging, but the result is stunning. I hope you'll give it a try with the colors of your choice.

MATERIALS

All yardages are based on 42"-wide fabric.

1/8 yard *each* of 16 batiks for blocks, sashing, and border*

2 1/8 yards of black fabric for blocks, sashing, borders, and binding

3 yards of fabric for backing

52" x 52" piece of batting

*I used 2 yellows, 2 golds, 2 peaches, 2 pinks, 2 lavenders, 2 blues, 2 teals, and 2 light greens for a total of 16 different batiks. One batik of each color was used for the horizontal rows of colors and the second batik of each color was used for the vertical rows. Decide which 8 fabrics will be vertical and which 8 fabrics will be horizontal before cutting.

CUTTING

From each of the 8 batiks for horizontal colors, cut:
- 2 strips, 1 1/2" x 42"; from the strips, cut:
    2 strips, 1 1/2" x 21"
    16 rectangles, 1 1/2" x 2 1/2"

From the black fabric, cut:
- 9 strips, 1 1/2" x 42"; crosscut each strip into 2 strips, 1 1/2" x 21" (1 is extra)
- 2 strips, 1 1/2" x 42"; crosscut into 9 rectangles, 1 1/2" x 8"
- 4 strips, 1 1/2" x 42"; crosscut into 4 strips, 1 1/2" x 32"
- 5 strips, 1 1/2" x 42"; crosscut into:
    72 squares, 1 1/2" x 1 1/2"
    8 rectangles, 1 1/2" x 3 1/2"
    8 rectangles, 1 1/2" x 2 1/2"
- 4 strips, 3 1/2" x 42"; crosscut into 4 strips, 3 1/2" x 33 1/2"
- 5 outer-border strips, 2 1/2" x 42"
- 5 binding strips, 2 1/2" x 42"

From each of the 8 batiks for vertical colors, cut:
- 2 strips, 1 1/2" x 42"; from the strips, cut:
    1 strip, 1 1/2" x 32"
    1 rectangle 1 1/2" x 8"
    16 rectangles, 1 1/2" x 2 1/2"

MAKING THE HORIZONTAL STRIP SETS

These strip sets create the colors that run horizontally across the quilt. When pieced into the quilt, however, the strips cut from the strip sets are vertical.

1. Label and number the horizontal fabrics H1 through H8. Begin with H1 for the color that you want at the outside of the quilt and end with H8 for the color that you want at the center.

2. Sew a black 1½" x 21" strip to a 1½" x 21" strip of H1, pressing the seam allowances toward the black. Repeat for H2 to H8.

Repeat for H2 to H8.

3. Sew the strip sets together, keeping the colors in order from 1 to 8, and press the seam allowances toward the black. Sew one additional black strip to the H8 strip as shown; press. Repeat to make a second strip set, but do not add the black strip to the H8 strip.

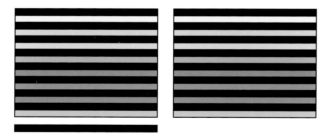

Make 1 of each.

4. Crosscut the strip sets every 1½" to create 11 horizontal strips from each strip set.

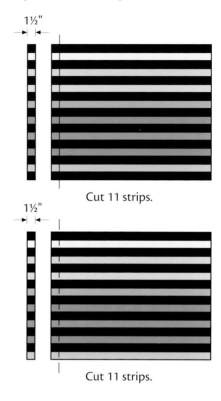

1½"

Cut 11 strips.

1½"

Cut 11 strips.

5. Place one horizontal strip from each strip set together by reversing one strip as shown so that both H8 colors are in the center. Sew the strips together to make a long horizontal strip. Repeat to make 11 strips.

Horizontal strip.
Make 11.

MAKING THE VERTICAL STRIP SETS

These strip sets create the colors that run vertically through the quilt. When pieced into the quilt, the strips will actually be horizontal.

1. Label your vertical fabrics beginning with V1 for the outer colors through V8 for the center colors, in the same order as the horizontal strips.

2. Sew a black 1½" x 8" rectangle to a 1½" x 8" rectangle of V1, pressing the seam allowances toward the black. Repeat for V2 through V8.

3. Sew the strip sets together, keeping the colors in order from V1 to V8, and press the seam allowances toward the black.

4. Sew one additional black strip to the V1 strip, pressing the seam allowances toward the black.

5. Crosscut the strip set every 1½" to create four vertical strips.

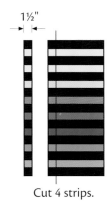

1½"

Cut 4 strips.

6. Place two vertical strips together as shown, reversing one strip so that both V8 colors are in the center. Remove one black square and sew together to make a long vertical strip. Repeat to make two.

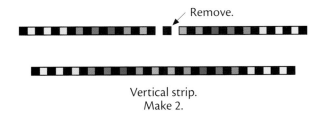

Remove.

Vertical strip.
Make 2.

MAKING THE SASHING STRIPS FOR VERTICAL COLORS

1. Sew 1½" x 32" strips of V1 and V2 to opposite sides of a black 1½" x 32" strip as shown. Press the seam allowances toward the black.

2. Crosscut the strip set every 1½" to create 18 sashing units.

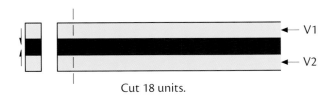

← V1
← V2

Cut 18 units.

3. In the same manner, sew strips of V3 and V4 to a black strip, strips of V5 and V6 to a black strip, and strips of V7 and V8 to a black strip. Press the seam allowances toward the black. Crosscut each strip set every 1½" to create 18 sashing units from each set.

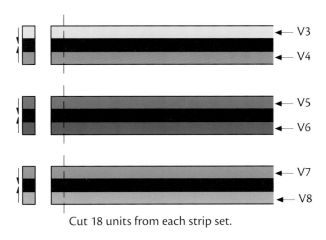

← V3
← V4

← V5
← V6

← V7
← V8

Cut 18 units from each strip set.

MAKING THE BLOCKS

1. Position 1½" x 2½" V1, V2, H1, and H2 rectangles around a black 1½" square as shown and sew together referring to "Partial Seams" on page 72. Press the seam allowances away from the center. Repeat to make two of this color combination.

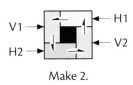

V1 →
H2 →
← H1
← V2

Make 2.

2. In the same manner, make two blocks in each of the 32 color combinations shown. You now have all the pieces needed to assemble the quilt top.

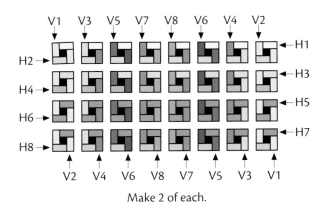

V1 V3 V5 V7 V8 V6 V4 V2

H2 →
H4 →
H6 →
H8 →

← H1
← H3
← H5
← H7

V2 V4 V6 V8 V7 V5 V3 V1

Make 2 of each.

QUILT-TOP ASSEMBLY

1. Referring to the diagram for proper orientation, lay out nine horizontal strip sets, the blocks, and the vertical sashing units in the correct positions. Remember that the horizontal strip sets are in a vertical position because they contain the horizontal colors.

2. Sew the blocks to the sashing units to create vertical rows. Press the seam allowances toward the blocks. Repeat to make eight rows.

3. Sew the vertical rows to the horizontal strip sets. Press the seam allowances toward the blocks. Your top should measure 33½" x 33½".

MAKING THE BORDER CORNER UNITS

1. Using the leftover batiks, cut 16 squares, 1½" x 1½", in a variety of colors.

2. Sew a batik 1½" square to a black 1½" x 3½" rectangle as shown. Press the seam allowance toward the black. Repeat to make eight units.

Make 8.

3. Sew a black 1½" square to one side of a 1½" batik square and sew a black 1½" x 2½" rectangle to the other side. Press the seam allowances toward the black. Repeat to make eight units.

Make 8.

4. Sew the units from steps 2 and 3 together, rotating them as shown. Press the seam allowances toward the units from step 1. Repeat to make eight units.

Make 8.

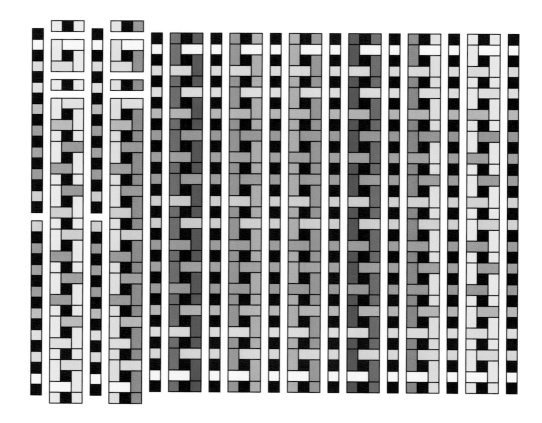

5. Sew two units from step 4 together as shown. Press the seam allowances in either direction. Repeat to make four corner units measuring 4½" x 4½".

Corner unit.
Make 4.

ADDING THE BORDERS

1. Lay out the top, the remaining vertical and horizontal strip sets, the black 3½" x 33½" inner-border strips, and the corner units, making sure they are rotated as shown.

2. Sew the strip sets to the border strips, pressing the seam allowances toward the border strips. Repeat for all four sides.

3. Sew the side border strips to each side of the quilt center, pressing the seam allowances toward the border strips.

4. Sew a corner unit to each end of the top and bottom border strips. Press the seam allowances toward the border strips.

5. Sew the top and bottom border strips to the quilt. Press seam allowances toward the borders.

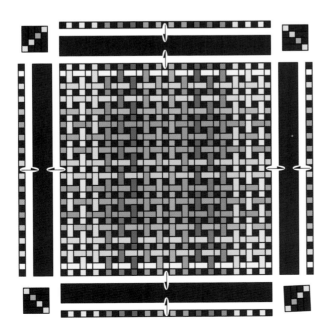

6. Refer to "Measuring Borders" on page 75. Piece and cut two black 2½"-wide strips and sew them to opposite sides of the quilt top. Press the seam allowances toward the border.

7. Measure, piece, and cut two 2½" black strips for the top and bottom edges. Sew them to the quilt top, and press the seam allowances toward the border strips.

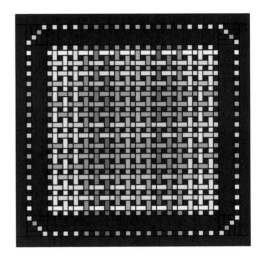

FINISHING THE QUILT

Refer to "Quiltmaking Basics" on page 76 as needed to complete the following steps.

1. Make a backing 3" to 5" larger on all sides than your quilt top.

2. Layer the quilt top with the batting and backing. Baste the layers together.

3. Quilt by hand or machine using the design of your choice.

4. Square up the quilt.

5. Prepare the binding and sew it to the quilt.

6. Add a label and a hanging sleeve, if desired, to complete your quilt.

QUILTING SUGGESTION

I quilted the center of this project by stitching in the ditch to enhance the woven effect. I used black thread for the black squares and invisible thread on the colored strips. The border areas are quilted in the curls-and-swirls design (shown on page 61) with black thread for a subtle look.

AUTUMN PATHS

Designed and made by Ilene Bartos.
Finished Quilt: 74½" x 94½"

One day as I was pondering rectangles, I realized that braids are simply rectangles with the ends cut off. With that as my launching point, I created this quilt using braids. In this design they weave over and under rectangles of focus fabric in autumn colors of browns, rusts, and gold. Placement of the lightest colors in the center of the quilt makes it look luminous and glowing.

MATERIALS

All yardages are based on 42"-wide fabric.

2⅞ yards of black fabric for inner and outer borders and flat-fold piping

2⅓ yards of focus fabric for quilt top and binding

⅜ yard *each* of 9 medium to medium-dark brown fabrics for interior and border braids

¼ yard *each* of 8 rust fabrics for interior and border braids

⅛ yard *each* of 6 gold fabrics for interior braids

¼ yard of dark brown fabric for interior and border braids

7 yards of fabric for backing

81" x 101" piece of batting

CUTTING

From the focus fabric, cut:
- 1 strip, 24½" x 42"; crosscut into:
    1 rectangle, 16½" x 24½"
    1 rectangle, 10½" x 24½"
    1 rectangle 6½" x 24½"
- 1 strip, 18½" x 42"; crosscut into:
    1 rectangle, 16½" x 18½"
    1 rectangle, 10½" x 18½"
    1 rectangle, 6½" x 18½"
- 1 strip, 10½" x 42"; crosscut into:
    1 rectangle, 10½" x 16½"
    1 square, 10½" x 10½"
    1 rectangle, 6½" x 10½"
- 9 strips, 2½" x 42"

From the dark brown fabric, cut:
- 4 squares, 5" x 5"; cut each square twice diagonally to make 16 triangles

From the 9 brown fabrics, cut:
- 16 strips, 3" x 42"; crosscut into 94 rectangles, 3" x 6½"
- 14 strips, 2½" x 42"; crosscut into 82 rectangles, 2½" x 6½"

From the 8 rust fabrics, cut:*
- 13 strips, 2½" x 42"; crosscut into 74 rectangles, 2½" x 6½"
- 14 strips, 2" x 42"; crosscut into 80 rectangles, 2" x 6½"

From the 6 gold fabrics, cut:*
- 14 strips, 1½" x 42"; crosscut into 84 rectangles, 1½" x 6½"

Save the remainders of your strips when cutting; use them for filling in along the top of the braids after they are trimmed.

From the black fabric, cut on the lengthwise grain:

- 2 strips, 3½" x 91"
- 2 strips, 3½" x 78"
- 2 strips, 3½" x 46½"
- 2 strips, 3½" x 40½"
- 2 strips, 3½" x 34½"
- 2 strips, 3½" x 30½"
- 2 strips, 3½" x 28½"
- 2 strips, 3½" x 24½"
- 2 strips, 3½" x 22½"
- 2 strips, 3½" x 16½"
- 1 strip, 1½" x 46½"
- 1 strip, 1½" x 40½"
- 1 strip, 1½" x 34½"
- 1 strip, 1½" x 28½"
- 1 strip, 1½" x 24½"
- 1 strip, 1½" x 18½"
- 1 strip, 1½" x 16½"
- 1 strip, 1½" x 10½"

MAKING THE BRAIDS

Refer to the following charts for braid length and the number of pieces of each color family to use. You will make one braid of each length; each braid also includes one triangle cut from the darkest brown fabric.

Interior Braid Length	Browns 2½" x 6½"	Rusts 2" x 6½"	Golds 1½" x 6½"
16½"	7	5	5
22½"	7	7	10
24½"	8	8	10
28½"	9	8	13
30½"	9	11	11
34½"	11	13	10
40½"	14	12	14
46½"	17	16	11

Border Braid Length	Browns 3" x 6½"	Rusts 2½" x 6½"
16½"	7	5
22½"	8	8
24½"	11	8
28½"	11	9
30½"	11	10
34½"	13	10
40½"	15	12
46½"	18	12

1. Begin with the shortest interior braid and gather the number of brown, rust, and gold rectangles as indicated in the chart. Arrange them from dark to light.

2. Sew the darkest brown rectangle to the left side of the dark brown triangle, starting at the 90° point of the triangle. Press the seam allowances toward the rectangle.

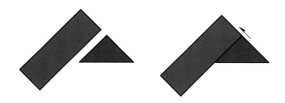

3. In the same manner, sew the next brown rectangle to the right side of the triangle. Press the seam allowances toward the newly added rectangle. Sew a third brown rectangle to the left side of the braid. Press the seam allowances toward the third rectangle. Continue in this manner, adding brown rectangles on alternating sides and pressing seam allowances toward the rectangle just added.

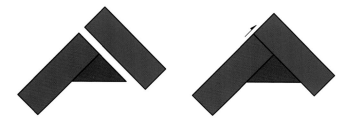

4. After all the brown rectangles have been added, trim the edges of the strip. First, trim across the bottom of the braid so that the rectangles are even with the bottom of the triangle. Then place a ruler over the braid, lining up the base of the ruler on the bottom and the 3¼" line of the ruler between the points of the braid as shown. Trim both sides of the braid and discard the triangles.

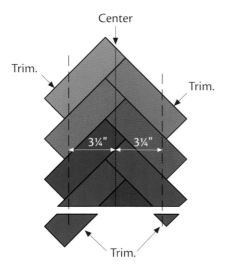

EASY TRIMMING

Use a ruler that is 6½" wide and place a strip of clear tape down the center of the ruler. Draw a heavy line on the tape to clearly mark the center of the ruler, 3¼" from each side. Align your drawn line between the points of the braid and trim each side.

5. Continue adding strips and trimming after each color until the braid is about 2" longer than the desired length. Trim off the top of the braid; using the extra pieces from cutting, add additional gold or rust pieces to the corners as needed. Trim and square up to the correct length. Repeat to make the 16 braids as indicated in the charts.

6. Sew a black 3½" strip of corresponding length to each side of the interior braids. Press the seam allowances toward the black strips.

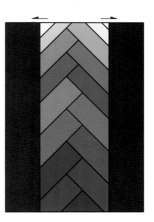

ASSEMBLING THE QUILT INTERIOR

1. Referring to the diagram, arrange the focus fabric rectangles and braids as shown, making sure the light gold section of each braid is placed toward the center of the quilt top. Sew together into four quadrants. Stop sewing 2" from the edge to create a partial seam wherever there is a circle. Refer to "Partial Seams" on page 72 for details.

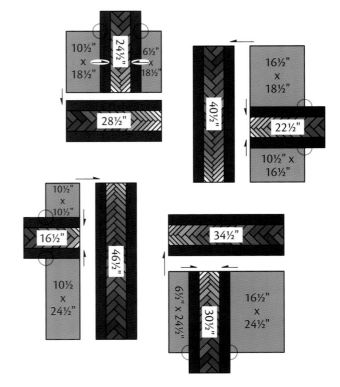

2. Sew the four quadrants to the 6½" x 10½" focus fabric rectangle in the order shown, starting with a partial seam as indicated by the circle. Finish the partial seam in the center only, leaving the ones on the outer border open.

MAKING THE FLAT-FOLD PIPING

1. Fold the black 1½"-wide strips of fabric in half lengthwise with wrong sides together and press.

2. Match each length of flat-fold piping with the corresponding edges of the quilt top. Align the raw edges and pin in place on each side. Overlap the strips at the corners. Refer to "Flat-Fold Piping" on page 74 for additional details, if needed.

ADDING THE BORDER BRAIDS

1. Making sure the light end of each border braid is toward the center of the top, sew the border braids to the quilt top, sandwiching the piping between

the border braids and the quilt top. Sew all layers together, beginning with the 28½" braid along the bottom left, then the 34½", 40½", and 46½" braids. Finish the partial seams.

2. In the same manner, sew the 16½", 22½", 24½", and 30½" braids and finish the partial seams.

ADDING THE OUTER BORDERS

1. Refer to "Measuring Borders" on page 75. Cut the two black 3½" x 91" border strips to fit and sew them to opposite sides of the quilt top. Press the seam allowances toward the borders.

2. Measure the quilt and cut the two 3½" x 78" black strips to fit. Sew these to the top and bottom edges of the quilt. Press the seam allowances toward the borders.

FINISHING THE QUILT

Refer to "Quiltmaking Basics" on page 76 as needed to complete the following steps.

1. Make a backing 3" to 5" larger on all sides than your quilt top.

2. Layer the quilt top with the batting and backing. Baste the layers together.

3. Quilt by hand or machine using the design of your choice.

4. Square up the quilt.

5. Prepare the binding and sew it to the quilt.

6. Add a label and a hanging sleeve, if desired, to complete your quilt.

QUILTING SUGGESTIONS

If you have a quilt with a busy focus fabric, it's a great place to practice a new quilting design such as the paisley I used, because mistakes really won't show. The braids are quilted with feathers in variegated thread. The black borders are quilted with a curls-and-swirls design stitched in black thread.

TREASURE BOXES

Designed and made by Ilene Bartos.
Finished Quilt: 20½" x 26½"

Have you ever purchased a gorgeous piece of hand-dyed fabric and then let it sit on the shelf for years because you were afraid to cut into it? This quilt was made with just such a piece. I cut sections of each color from a 3-yard piece of hand-dyed fabric, but the materials list includes five separate colors in case you don't want to cut up your hand-dyed fabric or you don't have one that is appropriate. Be sure to put a "treasure" into each of the smallest boxes—I've used bits of shells and skeleton leaves that were a gift from a special friend, Laura Cater-Woods.

MATERIALS

All yardages are based on 42"-wide fabric.

1/3 yard of green hand-dyed fabric for blocks

1/4 yard of red hand-dyed fabric for blocks

1/4 yard of orange hand-dyed fabric for blocks

1/4 yard of yellow hand-dyed fabric for blocks

1/4 yard of dark hand-dyed fabric for blocks

2/3 yard of fabric for backing

21" x 27" piece of batting

Optional embellishments:

1 skein of size 5 variegated pearl cotton

3 skeleton leaves (See "Resources" on page 79.)

4 large beads or shells

Misty-Fuse for attaching skeleton leaves

CUTTING

From the red fabric, cut:
- 1 strip, 2½" x 42"; crosscut into:
    1 rectangle, 2½" x 12½"
    2 rectangles, 2½" x 6½"
    1 square, 2½" x 2½"
    3 rectangles, 1½" x 2½"
- 1 rectangle, 3½" x 6½"
- 1 square, 4½" x 4½"

From the orange fabric, cut:
- 1 strip, 2½" x 42"; crosscut into:
    1 rectangle, 2½" x 8½"
    3 rectangles, 2½" x 4½"
    1 square, 2½" x 2½"
    2 rectangles, 1½" x 2½"
- 1 rectangle, 3½" x 10½"
- 1 rectangle, 4½" x 8½"

From the yellow fabric, cut:
- 1 strip, 2½" x 42"; crosscut into:
    1 rectangle, 2½" x 8½"
    2 rectangles, 2½" x 5½"
- 1 rectangle, 4½" x 8½"
- 3 rectangles, 1½" x 4½"

From the green fabric, cut:
- 1 strip, 2½" x 42"; crosscut into:
    1 rectangle, 2½" x 9½"
    2 rectangles, 2½" x 8½"
    2 rectangles, 2½" x 3½"
    1 rectangle, 1½" x 2½"
- 1 rectangle, 5½" x 6½"
- 1 rectangle, 4½" x 8½"
- 1 rectangle, 1½" x 9½"
- 1 rectangle, 1½" x 3½"

From the dark fabric, cut:

- 2 strips, 2½" x 42"; crosscut into:
    - 1 rectangle, 2½" x 12½"
    - 1 rectangle, 2½" x 8½"
    - 1 rectangle, 2½" x 6½"
    - 2 rectangles, 2½" x 4½"
    - 3 rectangles, 2½" x 3½"
    - 1 square, 2½" x 2½"
    - 2 rectangles, 1½" x 2½"
- 2 rectangles, 1½" x 3½"

MAKING THE BOX BLOCKS

1. Sew two orange 1½" x 2½" rectangles to a dark 1½" x 3½" rectangle, stopping about 1" from the left end of each to form a partial seam (indicated by circles). Refer to "Partial Seams" on page 72 if needed. Press the seam allowances toward the dark rectangle.

2. Sew the orange 3½" x 10½" rectangle to the right side of the unit from step 1. Press the seam allowances toward the orange rectangle.

3. Sew the green 1½" x 9½" rectangle to the dark 1½" x 3½" rectangle along the short edges; press the seam allowances toward the dark rectangle. Sew this strip to the top of the unit from step 2, pressing the seam allowances toward the unit. Repeat with the green 2½" x 9½" rectangle and the dark 2½" x 3½" rectangle, sewing the strip to the bottom of the unit.

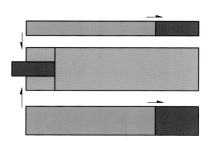

4. Sew the dark 2½" x 6½" rectangle to the right side of the unit. Press the seam allowances toward the dark rectangle.

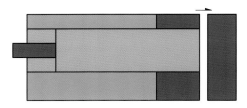

5. Sew the green 1½" x 2½" rectangle to the unit and then complete the partial seam. Repeat with the green 1½" x 3½" rectangle.

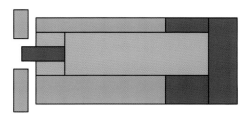

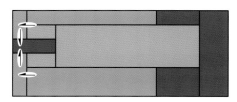

6. Sew the green 5½" x 6½" rectangle to the left of the unit to complete block A. Press the seam allowances toward the green rectangle. The block should measure 6½" x 20½".

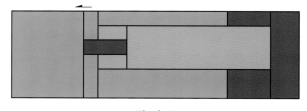

Block A

7. Repeat the sewing process for block B using yellow, red, and dark fabrics. Sew partial seams where indicated. The block should measure 8½" x 12½".

8. Repeat the sewing process for block C using orange, dark, and red fabrics. Sew partial seams where indicated. The block should measure 12½" x 12½".

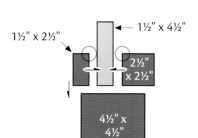

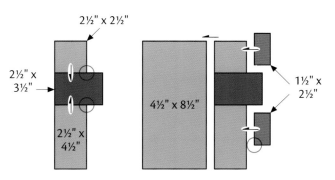

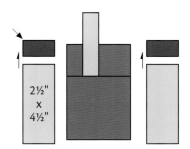

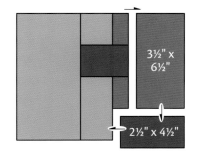

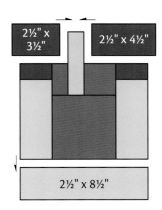

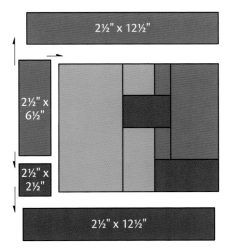

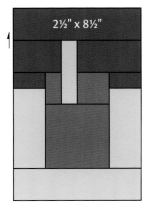

Block B

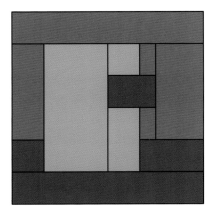

Block C

9. Repeat the process for block D using yellow, red, and green fabrics. The block should measure 8½" x 20½".

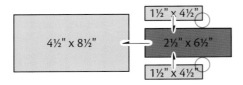

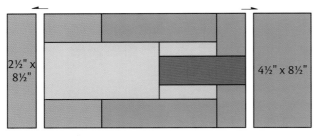

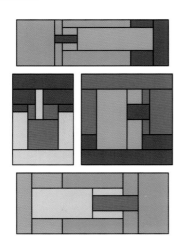

Block D

QUILT-TOP ASSEMBLY

1. Sew blocks B and C together. Press the seam allowances in either direction.

2. Sew block A to the top of the B-C unit, and sew block D to the bottom. Press seam allowances in either direction.

ADDING DETAILS

Big-stitch quilting serves as added embellishment on the quilt top. You can skip these steps if you prefer, adding the batting to the quilt sandwich in the next section.

1. Draw quilting lines on the top using a ruler and chalk. Refer to the photo on page 62.

2. Place batting under quilt top and baste the two layers together using a spray adhesive or pins.

3. With the cotton pearl floss and a needle, quilt through both the top and the batting. Use a long stitch on top and a short stitch on the bottom. This is sometimes called a utility stitch. Instead of making a knot, take a couple of short stitches in the batting on the back to avoid bulk.

FINISHING THE QUILT

1. Cut the backing the same size as the quilt top or slightly smaller and place it on top of the quilt, right sides together. Make a slit in the backing about 10" long and 2" from the top edge. With the batting on the bottom, next to the machine, sew a ¼" seam around all four sides of the quilt sandwich. Take one stitch on the diagonal when you come to the corners.

2. Trim the batting very close to the stitching and grade the seam. Turn the quilt right side out through the slit and gently push out the corners to make them square. Press the edges, making sure none of the backing shows on the front by turning it slightly toward the back. Use a whipstitch to sew the slit in the backing closed.

3. Referring to "Quiltmaking Basics" on page 76 as needed, quilt by hand or machine quilt using the design of your choice. I quilted in the ditch with invisible thread around each of the different colored sections.

4. Add a label and a hanging sleeve to complete your quilt. The sleeve will cover the slit in the backing.

5. Attach the skeleton leaves by using Misty-Fuse and a pressing cloth; follow the manufacturer's instructions.

6. Attach the shell beads with a needle using invisible thread.

TASJA'S SECRET ROSE GARDEN

Designed by Ilene Bartos with help from Natasja.
Pieced and quilted by Sally Morge, Las Cruces, New Mexico.
Finished Quilt: 57" x 54½"

My granddaughter, Natasja, drew a rose one day and I thought it was adorable, so I designed a quilt using her flower. The youthful colors were chosen to coordinate with the awesome print fabric used in the vertical panels. We are delighted to offer it here for you to enjoy.

MATERIALS

All yardages are based on 42"-wide fabric.

1¾ yards of focus fabric for panels

¼ yard *each* of 10 coordinating fabrics for pieced panels and appliqué

⅞ yard of blue fabric for center panel

½ yard of dark green fabric for accent strips and stems

½ yard of lime green fabric for binding

3½ yards of fabric for backing

61" x 63" piece of batting

1 skein of red embroidery floss for flowers

1 skein of black embroidery floss for butterflies

1 package of green medium rickrack for flowers

Batting scraps for flowers (optional)

CUTTING

Refer to the photograph on page 67 and placement diagrams on page 69 before cutting the 10 fabrics for the pieced panels. You may want to arrange the fabrics first to decide color placement before cutting.

From the 10 coordinating fabrics, cut a total of:
- 1 rectangle, 9½" x 7¾"
- 1 rectangle, 9" x 7¾"
- 8 rectangles, 6½" x 7¾"
- 1 rectangle, 6" x 7¾"
- 2 rectangles, 4½" x 7¾"
- 10 rectangles, 3½" x 7¾"

From the dark green fabric, cut:
- 6 strips, 1" x 42"
- ¾" bias strips to total 64"
- 8 bias strips, ¾" x 6½"

From the focus fabric, cut:
- 2 panels, 9½" x 54½", *on the* lengthwise *grain*
- 2 panels, 5½" x 54½", *on the* lengthwise *grain*

From the blue fabric, cut:
- 2 strips, 12½" x 42"; crosscut into two pieces, 12½" x 27½"

From the lime green fabric, cut:
- 6 strips, 2½" x 42"

MAKING THE PANELS

1. Sew together the 7¾"-wide pieces for panel A and panel B, referring to the assembly diagram below. Press the seam allowances in one direction.

2. Piece the 1"-wide dark green strips together and cut into two pieces, 54½" long. Sew one to each side of the A and B panels. Press the seam allowances toward the green strips.

3. Referring to the assembly diagram for correct placement, sew a 5½" focus fabric panel to one side of each pieced panel. Press the seam allowances toward the green strips. Sew a 9½" focus fabric panel to the other side of each pieced panel. Press the seam allowances toward the green strips.

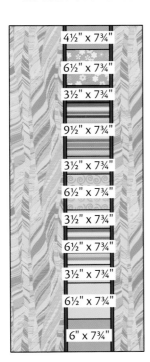

Panel A

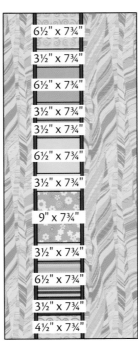

Panel B

4. Sew the two blue 12½" x 27½" panels together to make one panel, 12½" x 54½".

APPLIQUÉING THE CENTER PANEL

1. Referring to "Making Stems" on page 73, use the ¾" x 60" dark green bias strip to make the long stem. Use the eight ¾" x 6½" dark green bias strips to make the short stems.

2. Cut nine leaves on the bias from the dark green fabric, using the leaf patterns on page 71. Using the leftover panel fabrics, cut out nine flower fronts and nine flower backs on the bias in a variety of colors.

3. Fold the blue center panel in half lengthwise and make a crease to mark the center; fold in the opposite direction to find the horizontal center. Position and pin all the stems and leaves to the panel following the placement guide below and referring to the photo on page 67. Arrange the flowers on the background temporarily to make sure the stems are where you want them. Then remove the flowers and set them aside.

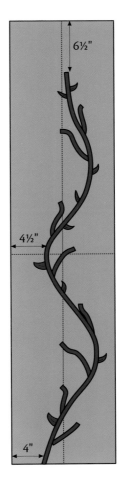

4. Use your favorite appliqué method or refer to "Appliqué Basics" on page 72 as needed. Appliqué the leaves first, and then the short stems. Stitch the long stem last, making sure to cover up the raw edges of the leaves and short stems.

5. Position and appliqué the flower backs first. You will not need to do the lower edge, as it will be covered up by the flower front.

6. Use three strands of red embroidery floss and embroider the swirls on the flower backs using a stem stitch. Refer to "Embroidery" on page 74 as needed.

7. Cut the green rickrack into 18 pieces of varying lengths from 3½" to 5½" long. Place the rickrack on both sides of the embroidered swirl; make sure you don't cover your embroidery. Attach the rickrack by taking a small appliqué stitch on each point.

8. Using the leftover panel fabrics, cut 18 circles and stitch them to the ends of the rickrack. Before taking the last few stitches, stuff the circles with a tiny amount of batting to make them puffy, if desired.

9. Appliqué the nine flower fronts, making sure to cover the raw edges of the flower backs and rickrack.

10. Cut out five hearts from the leftover fabrics. Appliqué a heart to each butterfly before cutting it out. Then cut and appliqué the butterfly to the center panel using your favorite method.

11. Use three strands of black embroidery floss to embroider around the center heart and to stem stitch the antennae.

QUILT-TOP ASSEMBLY

Sew panel A to the left side of the center panel, pressing the seam allowances toward panel A. Sew panel B to the right side of the center panel and press.

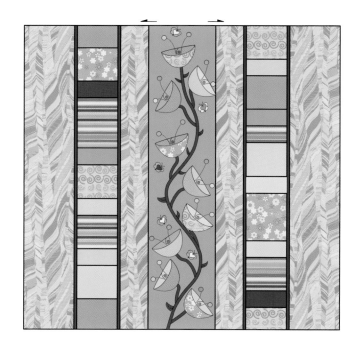

FINISHING THE QUILT

Refer to "Quiltmaking Basics" on page 76 as needed to complete the following steps.

1. Make a backing 3" to 5" larger on all sides than your quilt top.

2. Layer the quilt top with the batting and backing. Baste the layers together.

3. Quilt by hand or machine using the design of your choice.

4. Square up the quilt.

5. Prepare the binding and sew it to the quilt.

6. Add a label and a hanging sleeve, if desired, to complete your quilt.

QUILTING SUGGESTIONS

The center panel was quilted in a meandering stitch around the flowers, and each leaf received a vein line quilted down the center. The focus fabric is quilted on the lines of the fabric. The panels are each quilted in a different design with diamonds, squares, or swirls, based on the fabric motif.

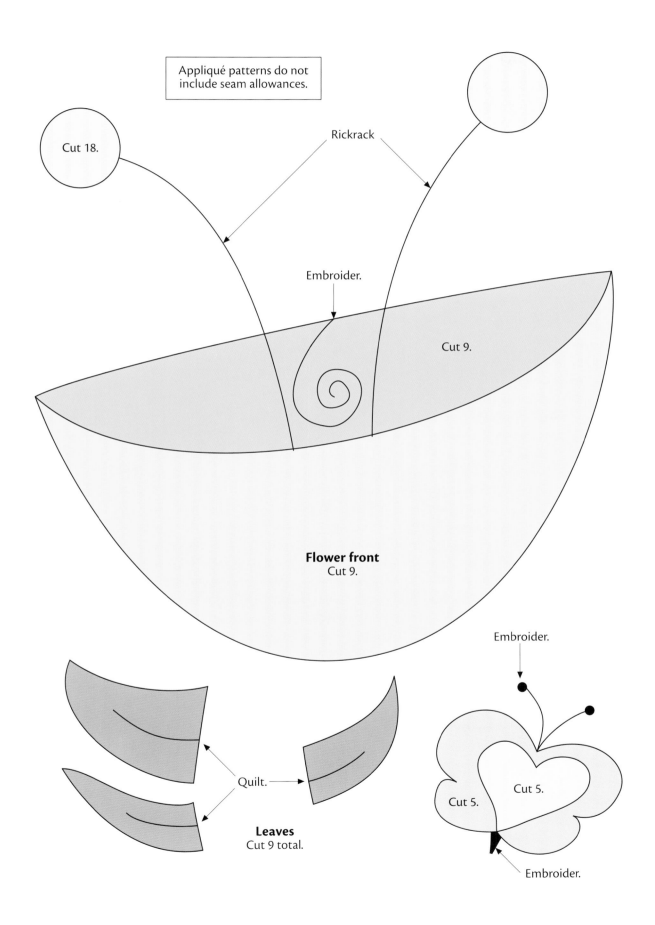

Appliqué patterns do not
include seam allowances.

Cut 18.

Rickrack

Embroider.

Cut 9.

Flower front
Cut 9.

Quilt.

Leaves
Cut 9 total.

Embroider.

Cut 5.

Cut 5.

Embroider.

QUILTMAKING BASICS

Refer to this section for details on partial seams, appliqué, making stems, embroidery, flat-fold piping, adding borders, and finishing your quilt.

PARTIAL SEAMS

If you've never tried the partial seam technique, you'll find it's an easy way to avoid sewing a difficult set-in seam. It's named very appropriately because you start with a seam that's only partially sewn, and then after adding other sections you finish by sewing together the unfinished, or partial, seam. If this sounds like an easy explanation, that's because it's an easy method to learn. Here is an example to give you a little practice.

1. Cut four rectangles, 4½" x 6½", and one center square, 2½" x 2½", from any fabric.

2. Place the square on the bottom right of rectangle 1 with right sides together. Sew from the bottom edge for about 1½", leaving about 1" not sewn. This is your partial seam. Press the seam allowances on the sewn section toward the rectangle.

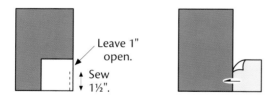

3. Sew rectangle 2 to the bottom of the unit. Press the seam allowances toward rectangle 2.

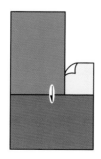

4. Repeat by adding rectangle 3 and rectangle 4, pressing the seam allowances toward the newly added rectangles.

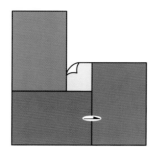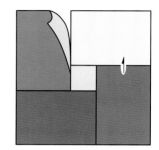

5. To finish the block, complete the partial seam, and press the seam allowances toward the first rectangle. The block will measure 10½" x 10½". Wasn't that easy?

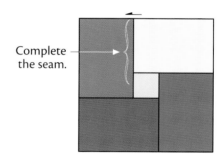

Complete the seam.

APPLIQUÉ BASICS

Appliqué is used to attach a piece of fabric onto a background. It's most commonly used for curved pieces and unusual shapes. The instructions given here are for a hand appliqué method called needle-turn appliqué. Of course, there are many different appliqué methods and you should feel free to use the method you're most comfortable with.

Making a Template

When doing appliqué you need a template to cut out your fabric. There are a variety of different template materials that can be used, but I suggest using freezer paper, which is inexpensive and readily available.

1. Cut out a piece of freezer paper slightly bigger on all sides than the appliqué pattern.

2. With the paper side up, lay the freezer paper over the pattern and trace the design with a dark pencil or permanent marker.

3. Cut out the shape on the drawn line. Make sure to cut with good scissors so you have edges that are even and straight. Jagged edges on your template will produce uneven appliqué pieces.

4. Press the freezer-paper template to the right side of the chosen fabric. The shiny side of the freezer paper will adhere to the fabric. Cut out the shape ¼" outside the edge of the template. This gives you enough extra fabric to turn under the edges. You may want to trim curved areas to approximately ⅛" to make them turn under easily.

Hand Appliqué

1. Place your fabric piece with freezer paper still attached on the background. Be sure to follow the order given in the pattern. Pin through the freezer paper and fabric with short appliqué pins to hold the shape in place.

2. Thread your needle with thread that matches the appliqué piece, not the background. I recommend very fine 60-weight cotton embroidery thread and a size 10 beading needle or size 11 straw needle. Make a small knot at the bottom of the thread.

3. Hold the piece with your nonsewing hand and use your needle to turn the seam allowance under the template. Finger-press and hold the turned-under seam allowance with your nonsewing hand. Bring the needle up through the background fabric and through the fold of the appliqué. The knot will be hidden underneath.

4. Insert the needle back down into the background right next to the fold, and bring the needle up into the fold again about ⅛" away. The stitch is similar to a blind hem stitch. Don't insert your needle into the background too far from the edge of the appliqué, or come up in the appliqué piece too far from the fold, or your stitches will show.

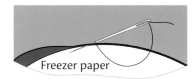

5. On curved areas you may want to clip the seam allowance to make a smooth curve. Clip with sharp scissors to within a couple threads of the template.

6. Continue making close stitches and turning under the seam allowance with the needle. Knot on the back when finished with a section and remove the template.

7. When doing a deep V, as in the heart, clip straight down in the V to within a thread and turn the first side under. Stitch to the point and take an extra stitch. Turn the piece so you can stitch up the other side, and sweep the seam allowance under with your needle, sweeping toward the V. Continue stitching.

Making Stems

Make stems with bias strips because they will curve nicely, unlike straight strips that do not curve (ask me how I know).

1. To make the bias strips, work with a piece of fabric that is about ½ yard. Trim both cut edges of your fabric so they are parallel to each other and a true 90° at the selvage edges. Fold one corner of your fabric over so that the selvage edge is aligned with the cut side of the fabric. The fold is now on the bias of the fabric.

2. Using a ruler, trim off a tiny bit at the fold, to eliminate the fold. Measure from the cut edge to cut strips. The 45°-angle line on your ruler should remain aligned with the trimmed edges of the fabric. Make cuts along the bias edge at the width needed

for your stems (in this project it's ¾") until you have the length you need.

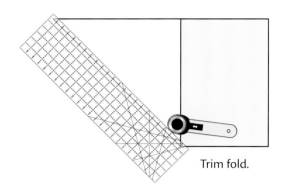

Trim fold.

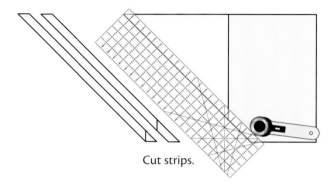

Cut strips.

3. Sew the strips together on the diagonal, offsetting the seams.

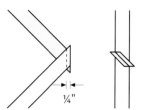

¼"

Press seam open.

4. Fold both raw edges under slightly less than ¼" on each side and press flat. One way to do this is to place straight pins into your pressing surface and run the folded stem fabric under the pins to help hold them in place until pressed flat. There are also stem-making tools on the market that can be used.

5. Once pressed, the stem is ready to be cut to the length needed and attached by pins to the background. It is then ready to appliqué in place using the method of your choice.

EMBROIDERY

Embroidery is like drawing on your quilt top by hand with needle and thread. You can also embroider using machine techniques.

1. To make a stem stitch, use three strands of embroidery floss. Knot the thread or take a few short stitches on the back, and come up through the background fabric at 1. Hold the thread below the needle with your thumb.

2. Go down at 2 and come up at 3. Take your next stitch by going down at 1 and coming back up at 4. Always hold your thread down below the needle.

3. When finished stitching, make a knot on the back or take a few short stitches to secure the thread.

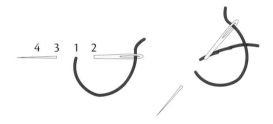

FLAT-FOLD PIPING

Regular piping is stuffed with cording to give it dimension, such as that used around a throw pillow. Flat-fold piping eliminates the use of cording, so it is very easy to make and gives your quilt an additional hint of color. You can add it as an accent between the center of the quilt and the outer border, or it can be sewn on the outer edge, just before adding the binding.

Flat-fold piping can be any width you want, but I often use a ¾"-wide strip, which results in ⅛" of fabric showing after it is sewn. This size can add an interesting and impressive accent, and it looks much harder than it actually is. "Autumn Paths" on page 56 uses a 1½"-wide piping for even more definition.

1. Cut four strips of fabric, ¾" wide by the lengths needed (length and width of your quilt). I usually add an extra inch to the length for ease in sewing. Make a separate piping strip for each edge of the quilt, piecing the strip if needed using a diagonal seam.

2. Fold each strip in half lengthwise with the *wrong* sides together, and press flat. The trick is to make sure the raw edges match exactly for the best results.

3. Starting with a side strip, pin the raw edges of the piping strip to raw edge of one side of the quilt top. Sew using a seam allowance slightly smaller than ¼" to avoid having to remove any stitches. Trim the ends of the strip even with the edges of the quilt top. Repeat for the opposite side.

4. Sew a piping strip to both the top and bottom edges of the quilt. Overlap the side piping in the corners. Trim the strips even with the edges of the quilt top.

MEASURING BORDERS

Measuring your quilt top before cutting borders is an important step; if the border is longer on one side of the quilt than on the other, you will end up with a lopsided quilt. If you don't measure at all and just sew on a length of fabric and then trim it, you are likely to create a wavy border. But, if you measure correctly, you can ease the quilt into the size it should be, if necessary, and keep it flat.

1. Measure the quilt through the center from top to bottom in three different places, and write down the measurements. Do not measure at the outside edges, because they may have stretched during handling. If your measurements are different, add the three numbers together and divide by three to determine the average. In the illustration, the three measurements were 40½", 40⅝", and 40⅜". The average is 40½", so that is the size to use when cutting the side border strips.

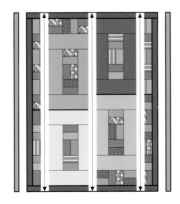

2. Sew a border strip to each side of the quilt top. Pin as needed to make sure the quilt top and border are sewn together evenly. You may have to stretch the fabric slightly or ease it in as you are sewing to make everything fit perfectly. Press the seam allowances toward the border strip.

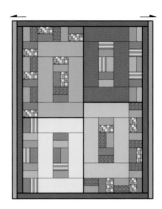

3. To determine the size to cut the top and bottom border strips, measure the quilt through the center from side to side, including the borders just added, in three different places, and write down the measurements. Use the average measurement and cut two border strips, one for the top and one for the bottom.

4. Sew a border strip to both the top and bottom edges of the quilt top, pinning as needed to ease in any extra fabric. Press the seam allowances toward the border strip.

MAKING THE BACKING

The quilt backing should be 3" to 5" larger than the quilt top on each side to allow for ease during quilting. The easy math method is to add 10" to the dimensions of your quilt top to determine the size to make your quilt backing. If your quilt top is 60" x 64", simply add 10" to each measurement and piece a backing measuring 70" x 74".

If you plan to do hand quilting, use as few seams as possible in the backing. If you are going to machine quilt, it really doesn't matter how much piecing you do.

The traditional method is to use lengths of fabric and sew them together with either vertical or horizontal seams to create the backing. Construct the backing to make the most efficient use of your fabric.

I like to piece the center of my backing by using up the leftover fabric pieces from the top. I surround it with borders in the width needed to make it large enough. This eliminates adding items to my scrap pile, and it makes an interesting backing. I wouldn't recommend this type of backing for hand quilting, though, because of all the extra seams.

LAYERING AND BASTING

Once you've completed the backing, layer the top, batting, and backing together in preparation for quilting.

1. Always iron the top and backing to get everything as flat and wrinkle-free as possible. If you are machine quilting, I recommend at least one application of spray starch.

2. Pin or tape the backing right side down onto a floor or table (or two tables pushed together). Stretch it to make it taut, and start pinning or taping in the center of each side and working toward the corners.

3. Cut a piece of batting slightly smaller than the backing and lay it on top of the backing.

4. Add the ironed quilt top, right side up, to the batting. Smooth it out, making sure that all visibly straight lines such as the inner border are straight.

5. Baste with thread in diagonal lines through all three layers for hand quilting, or pin baste by inserting small safety pins every few inches across the whole top for machine quilting. Pin through all three layers, starting in the center and working outward. I have also had success using a spray adhesive for this step.

6. Detach the quilt backing from the floor or table and you are ready to quilt.

BINDING

Once the quilting is finished, trim the quilt and square up the corners. Use a square ruler in the corners of the quilt and cut away the extra batting and backing using an accurate 90° angle. Cut the batting and backing slightly outside the edges of the quilt top if you are using a narrow binding. If you are using a wider binding, you may want to leave as much as 1/2" of batting and backing outside the quilt top to make sure you will have a full binding. I always measure the sides of the quilt top to make sure both sides and the top and bottom are trimmed to exactly the same length. If they aren't the same length, this is the time to even them up.

The binding needs to be a continuous strip at least 12" longer than the total of all four sides of your quilt top. It can be constructed of one fabric, or you can combine fabrics for a scrappy look.

The width of the binding can vary with each project and each quilter. You may want to experiment with different widths to determine your favorite. I personally like to use 2"-wide binding strips, resulting in a narrow 1/4" finished binding. But many quilters like to use either 2 1/4"- or 2 1/2"-wide strips. Most of the cutting instructions for the projects in this book list 2 1/2"-wide binding strips, but you can cut whatever width you prefer. "Ziggy Zaggy" on page 12 uses 3 1/2"-wide binding strips.

1. Cut as many strips of binding fabric as needed to get the total length required in the width you prefer.

2. Cut off the selvage edges and sew the strips together using a diagonal seam as shown. Press diagonal seam allowances open to avoid bulk.

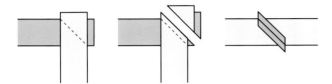

3. Press the entire binding strip in half lengthwise with the wrong sides together. Wrap the binding around an empty paper towel roll if desired to help make it manageable to work with.

4. Start in the center of one side, leaving a 10" tail. Align the raw edges of the binding with the trimmed edge of the quilt. Sew, using a walking foot if you have one. I use a ³/₈" seam allowance for my 2"-wide binding strips.

5. When you get to a corner, stop sewing ³/₈" from the corner and do a couple of backstitches. Remove the quilt from the machine and rotate it a quarter turn. Fold the binding straight up to create a miter as shown. Fold it back straight down. Make sure the fold is even with the edge of the quilt top, leaving the corner mitered and aligning the raw edges with the next edge to be sewn.

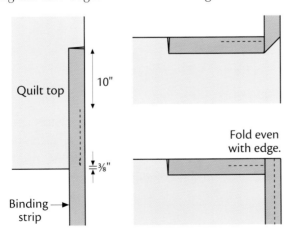

Quilt top

10"

Binding strip

³/₈"

Fold even with edge.

6. Continue sewing on the binding, starting at the edge of the fabric and continuing until you are ³/₈" from the next corner. Repeat the mitering at each corner. When you get to within 10" from where you started sewing, take a few backstitches and remove the quilt from the machine.

7. Fold the original 10" tail in half so you have a double layer that is 5" in length, and finger-press the fold. Take the remainder of the binding from the other side and fold it so that it is ¼" from the first fold as shown and finger-press the fold.

8. Unfold the original tail and mark the fold lines with a pencil on the wrong side of the fabric. Using a small ruler with a 45° line, align the 45° line along the edge of the binding strip as shown, so that the edge of the ruler is exactly on the X you marked. With a pencil, draw the diagonal line along the edge of the ruler. Trim the strip ¼" outside of the diagonal line.

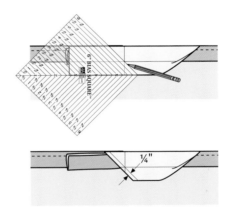

¼"

Trim, adding ¼".

9. Repeat with the end of the binding strip, making sure to draw a matching diagonal line and trimming ¼" from the line as shown.

¼"

Trim, adding ¼".

10. Fold the quilt and put a few pins in it to hold it together while sewing the diagonal seam. With right sides together as shown, pin and sew the seam, removing the pins as you sew. Finger-press the seam allowances open and continue sewing the binding

to the quilt top. Once this is done, you won't be able to tell where your binding starts or stops.

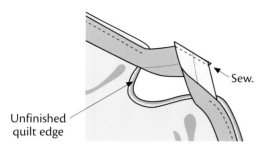

Unfinished quilt edge

Sew.

11. Fold the binding to the back of the quilt so that it just covers the stitching. Whipstitch the folded edge of the binding to the backing fabric using small stitches and a thread color that matches the binding fabric. Fold and stitch the miters at the corners as you get to them.

APPLYING A HANGING SLEEVE

There are so many ways to display quilts around your home. You can use them on your bed, arrange them on the back of your couch, drape them on a chair, or hang them on a quilt rack. One of my favorite ways is to fold them and showcase them on the shelves of an armoire. You can never have too many quilts!

To hang a quilt on a wall, add a sleeve on the back to hold the rod and allow the quilt to hang evenly. Quilts entered in shows must usually have a hanging sleeve. These dimensions will work for most quilt shows.

1. Cut a piece of muslin, or fabric that matches your backing, 8" wide by the width of your quilt top.

2. On each end, with the wrong side facing up, fold under ½", and then fold under another ½"; stitch by machine to finish the ends of the sleeve.

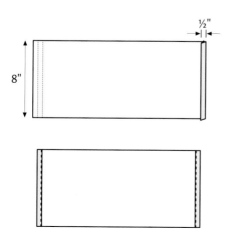

½"

8"

3. If you haven't yet applied the binding, you can attach the sleeve at the same time by folding wrong sides together and aligning the raw edges with the top of the quilt. Baste it in place. The raw edges will be covered when you apply your binding. Your tube should be 4" wide and 1" shorter than the quilt on both sides.

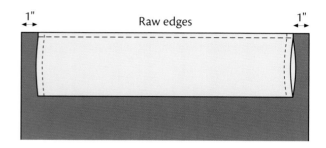

1" Raw edges 1"

If you apply your sleeve after you've bound the quilt, you'll need to sew it into a tube. Press the seam allowances open and hide it in the center of the back next to the quilt. Whipstitch the top close to the binding.

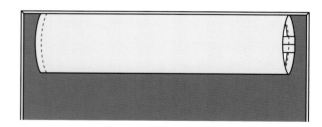

4. To make room for the rod, you need to fold the tube up by ½" and press. Whipstitch the bottom of the tube 3½" from the top of the quilt with a matching thread. The extra fabric will hold the rod as shown.

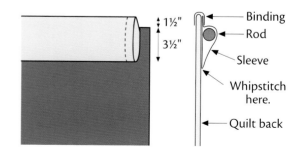

1½"

3½"

Binding
Rod
Sleeve
Whipstitch here.
Quilt back

ACKNOWLEDGMENTS

I want to especially thank my family, because without their understanding, support, and love, it would have been hard to find time to quilt and impossible to complete this book. My husband, Ron, generously puts up with my lack of time or desire to cook and clean, and has a good eye for design when I ask his opinion while creating a quilt. My children, Nikki, Ben, and Jessica, know to look for me in my studio when they visit—and to schedule time to do things with me ahead of time, giving me the freedom to finish projects. My wonderful grandchildren, Natasja and Tanner, not only look for me in the studio, but spend time with me there—sometimes designing or sewing, but often just watching movies with me while I sew. Thank you for being the best family ever.

For the quilting designs shown throughout the book, I'd like to acknowledge a wonderful teacher, Nicole Rivera. I took a machine-quilting class from her a few years ago; her designs and techniques really clicked with me. In fact, they became so natural for me that it's really hard to tell what designs are totally hers and which ones are totally mine. We are both very happy to share the designs I've used in this book. You can contact Nicole at her email address, yesyoucanquilt@gmail.com. I highly recommend her books or classes.

I'd also like to thank my twin sister, Lorene Harris, who comes over and sews with me every Sunday afternoon. She has helped me in a variety of ways, including but not limited to listening to me at length when I didn't think I could make a deadline. Thanks so much for your support; I appreciate you and value our relationship, which has grown through quilting together.

Finally, I'd like to acknowledge all of my wonderful quilting friends; without your collective support, knowledge, and gentle pushes, I wouldn't be writing this today. You probably have no clue how vital your friendships have been to my development as a fiber artist, but I wouldn't be here without you. I hope to spend many more years walking down the road of life with you, growing better together, supporting each other when needed, and just enjoying our friendship and time together.

RESOURCES

Quarter Circle Template Set

Available from the author at www.ilenebartos.com

Skeleton Leaves

Available from art supply stores,
Laura Cater-Woods at www.cater-woods.com,
and www.ArtisticArtifacts.com

ABOUT THE AUTHOR

Ilene Bartos has always enjoyed creating—art was her favorite class in school. When she discovered quilting a number of years ago, it was the perfect medium for her creative outlet. It combines color with a process that is very relaxing and can be done in the evenings after a hard day of work. Also, quilts have a longevity that isn't found in a lot of other mediums, as they are treasured now and for years to come. She lives with her husband, Ron, in Urbandale, Iowa, and enjoys her three children and two grandchildren who live nearby and visit often. She loves to travel and share her quilting experiences and techniques with others. *Spectacular Rectangles* is her second book.

THERE'S MORE ONLINE!

See more of Ilene Bartos's work and her teaching schedule at www.IleneBartos.com. Find more great books about quilting, knitting, crochet, and more at www.martingale-pub.com.